From August to Infinity

A Memoir

By Mary Bosley & Morgan Przybylski

Enjoy!
Mary Bosley Morgan Przybylski

PublishAmerica
Baltimore

First printing

PublishAmerica has allowed this work to remain exactly as the author intended, verbatim, without editorial input.

ISBN: 978-1-4489-5103-1
PUBLISHED BY PUBLISHAMERICA, LLLP
www.publishamerica.com
Baltimore

Printed in the United States of America

From Mary:

Dedicated to my PopPop
"All I know about us is that beautiful things never last, that's why fireflies flash"
—Ron Pope

From Morgan:

This memoir is for all the people who have suffered in their lives, especially those who have suffered abuse. This is my hope that you will empower yourselves to get out. You deserve better and can have more.

"Nobody can go back and start a new beginning, but anyone can start today and make a new ending." —Maria Robinson.

I dare you all to change your ending into a better one.

Preface via Mary

Okay, so let's start with the basics so I can attempt to make things interesting, and perhaps even provide you with a few "aw" moments.

How it began is still a mystery to me, I was a know-it-all fifteen year old girl, whose heart was hardened, and whose general cynicism drove people away faster than a monkey in a dolphin shop. I didn't care about the world around me, and thought that I was being punished by God for things I didn't even do. Nonetheless I found myself in a familiar place, with the same people I'd been vacationing with since before I could remember. Only this time I had just broken up with bad decision number 3,021, and I was less than amused by the fact that I had to entertain the people I'd grown up with for yet another week under that same stupid tent on that oh so familiar beach. As much as I'd complained I distinctly remember what it felt like to get to a place that actually felt like home. That place, you ask?

Sunset Beach, North Carolina. Which conveniently enough is located on a barrier island known as Sunset Island. You see, at the southern most point of North Carolina is where it lies, and although few know it, those who have the privilege to be enamored by its charm can't help but fall hard. To actually get to this little slice of paradise requires not only great luck, but much patience incase Lady Luck isn't on your side. If you can survive the maze of back roads, you'll soon find that you come to a one-lane wooden swing bridge, that's where Lady Luck comes in because if you don't get the green light to go across, you will have fun sitting in traffic for the next twenty to forty five minutes, depending on how much traffic there is, and of course, the time of day. As time elapses the world seems to go with it, and unfortunately you won't need luck or back roads any more because by the time you read this they will have torn down the old bridge and erect a new one that connects to the main land. Though I'll never be able to picture Sunset Island as touristy and popular, the owners had bigger plans. The charm of the Island may be in jeopardy, yet it still warms my soul to remember the quaint and quiet summers I'd spent there, and maybe it will even help me to look forward to those summers that have yet to come.

So let's get down to the facts. Sunset Island measures up to a whopping mile wide, and two whole miles long, its "perks" if you will include; an arcade, an ice cream shop, a general store, and a few beach-esque stores. Other than that there are houses surrounded by the ocean on one side, and the bay on the others. Though it doesn't sound like much, for me it was more than enough. The other key element to Sunset Beach is known as the Kindred Spirit. This, as those who go to the island believe, is a force if you will that protects and brings luck to those on the island. Many believe that it not only protects those on the island but it also brings luck and in some cases love. There is even a mailbox where you can write letters to the Kindred Spirit for luck and love. Overall Sunset Beach's humble and rather quaint atmosphere and calming ocean view are just some of the reasons why I've been going back ever since I was three. Okay, so maybe it wasn't my choice when I was younger but laying here now, the night before I start my freshman year of college, I am certain that I wouldn't have it any other way.

I write this story for a few simple reasons, first and most importantly, I believe everyone has a story to tell. This is my first, but hopefully not my last. I'll let you decide. Secondly, where I am in the story, Myrtle Beach, SC, as you'll find out due to my grandfather, who passed away in 2002, so this story is my way of paying him homage for giving me something that not everyone has, a home away from home. A place to come and rest. A place to think and better myself, and for that I am forever grateful. I write this story with much care and thought, this is my life, and my soul. I hope you can take it for what it is, and maybe even learn something.

When writing I know I have a tendency to jump around, hopefully most of that gets eliminated in the editing, but if not just bear with me. I promise it'll all make sense in the end. You'll also notice I have a tendency to talk right to you, to use inclusive language, so you can feel like you were there too. It's my style, I hope you like it! With this story being told from two different points of view you may find that there are discrepancies but that's because we are remembering it the way we know it. Though it may seem contradictory at times, we would rather tell the story, as we know it rather than doctoring it to make it match up. Spoiler: the only big mismatch is the day that we met the boys, I have when we met them a day later than her, but that's how I remember it and Morgan remembers it her way. Either way it doesn't matter, what matters is that we did, in fact, meet them. With all of that being said, I guess there is just one last thing to say before we begin:

This story that I am about to delve into with you is the truth, as I know it. Some of the details may seem too in depth considering the amount of time that has passed between the events and when this was being written; however I have kept journals dating back to three days after I got home from this particular trip and have drawn from those entries to keep the story as authentic as possible. As for some of the earlier dialogue, it may not be verbatim but I know these people, I love them and talk to them just about every day. I know how they talk and because of that I was able to create a dialect that is true to their nature. Where this preface ends, my story begins. The year was 2005, I was fifteen, and completely oblivious to what was in store for me on a small island in North Carolina, during the first week of August.

Preface Morgan Style

Sometimes in life someone comes into your life and changes everything. For me this happened when I was just fourteen years old. His name was Zack.

Let me tell you a little about myself before we get started. My name is Morgan Przybylski. Crazy last name, I know, but that's not important. I'm 18 years old and about to be a freshman in college. I live in Baltimore, MD. I have a crazy family that is very much involved in my life, but you know I wouldn't have it any other way. I have an older sister, Ashley, and a younger brother RJ. My parents are incredible. My mom is like my best friend. She's one of those moms that you can tell anything, but she will still be a mom to you and she will always listen. My dad is sarcastic and critical, but only because he loves you so much he wants to fix you, I guess.

My story begins four years ago, in 2005. I was just fourteen years old. At the time I was literally just getting out of an abusive relationship. I can't say he ever hit me, but I would definitely say it was emotional abuse and pushed me into things that I wasn't ready for. He didn't care what I thought or felt. It was just about making him happy. He had me wrapped around his finger, and he knew it. This guy was still in my life. He was trying to get back with me and I was on the verge of giving into his persuasion. I just couldn't see the fact that it was not normal. I had never known anything else. Thankfully before we could get back together, I went to on vacation to Sunset Beach.

Maybe I should give you a little background information. Now my family has been going to Sunset Beach, North Carolina for as long as I can remember. Sunset Beach is a small barrier island in North Carolina; it's actually the southern most beach in North Carolina. It measures up to one mile in width and two miles in length. The island is very quiet. There are six stores on the whole island. There is an arcade, bike shop, small grocery store, surf shop, and all the rest are little tourist shops. The only way onto the island is by a single lane swing bridge.

Now this bridge is like the Eiffel tower is to France. It's the thing that makes it special. It was one lane sitting at the light is inevitable. Even worse, every hour on the hour the bridge swings open so that boats that can't fit under it can get through the canal. Yes, it is inconvenient and not emergency practical, but it shows the humility of the island. It shows that this place isn't just like everywhere else. It's not about going places and doing everything. It's about staying home, relaxing, spending time with family and friends, and most importantly, escaping the stresses of the rest of the world. The island hasn't been corrupted by the modern world. There are no supermarkets or malls. It's just the bare necessities: the rest you can get off the island. It is the perfect place. This bridge tells me everything about this place, and because of that I know it is the right place for me.

The bridge has always been my favorite part of the island. Unfortunately they are in the process of replacing the old bridge with a more convenient new bridge. It should be done by the time I go down there this year. When my mom told me the news I can't lie, I ran into my room and cried for hours. Who cries over bridges?! But in my mind everything will change, the whole place will be different, maybe even tainted.

I have faith, though. I have to believe in my heart that with or without this bridge the island will stay the same. I must still trust that it will be the ever relaxing, calming positive aroma that it is. There is just something special you feel as soon as you step onto the island. It is like a sense of relief or comfort or maybe even safety. I'm beginning to become more confident that nothing will change that. Why? The Kindred Spirit.

Sunset Beach has something no other island has, the Kindred Spirit. The Kindred Spirit is the thing that everyone writes to in the mail box on Bird Island. But what is this Kindred Spirit? Everyone has a different opinion of this so-called spirit. Some say it is some sort of luck. Others say that it watches over the island to make sure that no harm is down to the precious land or occupants. Yet, my favorite description must be the one that was given to me by my sister Ashley. She believes that "It brings people together. It is like a lure. I mean, its like destiny. I know that without it we would not have met the people that we have met, and we would not be the people that we are." I personally think that it is a combination of them all. I am a strong believer in the Kindred Spirit and always will be. It is the reason for my story. It is the backbone that allowed all of this to happen. Kindred Spirit, I thank you.

Maybe the reason I love this beach so much is because I love the people I go there with. We go with about 30 people. Don't worry I'm pretty sure Mary names them at some point, so I won't waste your time right now.

So like I was saying I was in an abusive relationship. I really didn't know how to get out of it either. I was sure I was on the fast track to nowhere and if I had stayed, I would have ended up pregnant or something. The only way I thought I could get out was to meet someone new and tell him it was over. That was my plan too. I was going to meet someone, talk to them, and maybe even hook up with them. After all that I'd go tell the other guy, Jeff, that I was in love with this new guy, even if I wasn't. Pretty good plan right? The only thing was he had a temper, so it was kind of risking it. So that's how the week started. Little did I know I would still be thinking about it four years later. That's what it does to you, love that is. It comes up unexpectedly, and it never leaves you. Kind of like herpes, just kidding! Keep in mind; Sunset beach is so small the only way onto it is from a one-lane swing bridge, so the chance of meeting someone is slim. But this was different.

Via Mary
Monday, Day 0
Chapter One: Thoughts

"Are we there yet??" Ah yes the question on every child's mind when going on long trips. At fifteen, I of course, didn't view myself as a child, but hey whose to say the question didn't cross my mind once or twice...or five hundred times?

Allow me to introduce myself. I'm Mary, and I was lucky enough to embark upon the trip from hell also known as the eight and a half hour car ride down to our other house in North Myrtle Beach, SC. I guess I should be used to the car ride by now but I can't help but get jittery once we hit a certain point in NC. I guess I should give you a history lesson on who "we" are and why we venture down to SC every year for a few weeks.

On my father's side are six very important people, my grandmother (MomMom), my grandfather (PopPop), my Uncle Richard, my Aunt Judy, and my cousins Sara and Patrick, and to make that family complete feel free to add in my dad (Joe), my mom (Cathy), my brother (Erik), and of course me! My PopPop as I lovingly refer to him, was my only grandfather that I met, and he made sure his grandchildren were always happy. In fact that's how we wound up in SC to begin with. Our birth order is as follows: Erik, Myself, Sara, and Patrick. Patrick is pretty great, but not important enough because by the time Sara came around our PopPop decided to get a house in SC so his grandchildren would always have a place to go on vacation. Now I say Patrick doesn't matter in a loving way because he's great: he just wasn't born in time.

So ever since I was three, I've been going there. This particular trip, however, was a little bit hard. I had just broken up with Brandon or shall I say he broke up with me. Not that it matters. I didn't like him that much anyway it was just something to pass the time. I'm selfish, I know. I'm also a bit abrasive at times. I'm not worried though; you'll learn to love me. In any event, all of this doesn't change the fact that I was stuck in a car with my brother, and my parents listening to the millionth country song about how some guy got left by his wife and his dog got ran over by a truck…or something. That's not the point. The point is even though I was hot, cranky and generally not happy to be in the car with family members that are a bit excessive in the noise department, I got to do some thinking. And let me tell you, I tend to think myself in circles, but every time I do I always came back to this one major thought…

I want to be compelling. I want someone to be so drawn to me that no matter how far away he was, he would still want to know about how I am, and what I am up to. I want someone to crave my presence in his life; I want someone to want me as bad as I want him. I realize now that all I did was lower my standards because I never realized that I was worth something. I don't mean to come off as arrogant, but my self worth has always be a huge question mark and these eight and half hours of serious thinking time were beginning to make it into an exclamation point or at the very least a period. As much as I want someone to feel all of those things about me, I'm not sure that I can risk the heartbreak again. Yes I know, if I find the right person there won't be any need for heartbreak. Either way this vacation is going to be boy-free. This vacation is going to be for me.

I remember wondering what Morgan was up to; at that point I was willing to bet that they hadn't even left yet. You know how you have that one friend who no matter how many times you remind them as to what time an event is happening, they still show up late? Then you think you can be coy and do the whole bit where you tell them an hour early. Well with the Przybylski's, and I say this with love, you may as well tell them a few days early that way they show up on time. But I digress, I think the reason I wondered about Morgan is because I was worried about her. I wanted to know that she was doing all right, and not beating herself up over Jeff. You see Morgan is my best friend and my cousin, and she's probably one of the most amazing girls I know except for the fact that she doesn't believe she's good enough. It's almost painful to listen to her put herself down when she has such beauty both inside and out. Anyways she had her first serious boyfriend, and all he did was mess with her head. After the whole Jeff ordeal we both agreed that this vacation would be boy-free. This vacation called for some serious girl time, time we were going to use it to get back on our feet.

Aside from all of the self-righteous healing I planned on doing, I remember being worried about having to deal with the rest of our herd if you will. I use the word herd in all seriousness too. When we vacation, our group is made of thirty people; obviously we enjoy solitude on our family vacations! Along with my family of four there are: Uncle Richard, Aunt Judy, Sara, Patrick (aka the other Bosley's). That's just our house. In my best friend Morgan's house there is her dad, my Uncle Bobby, Aunt Laurie, Ashley, and RJ. Also in that house are Uncle Bobby's parents, Big Bob and Eva, Robin (Uncle Bobby's sister), her husband Jim and their son, Nick. In the next house there is Big Bob's best friend GW, his wife, Nancy, their son, John, his wife, Deb, and their two sons, Kyle and Jamie. Finally, in the last house there are Mr. Rosie, his wife Nancy, their children Amy and Scottie, and their friends Becky and Jon. If you thought that was confusing just wait for the rest of the book. You see my Uncle Richard isn't exactly the shyest guy around, so as you could guess our group tends to get bigger. Though he's not the only one to blame because if it hadn't been for the social skills that Morgan and I possess (or pure dumb luck, I'll let you decide) this book would have never been written. Oh and by the way I kind of wasted 45 seconds of your life because although the people I was with are very important, the two main people have yet to even be named. So in the interest of time, let's get to it.

Via Morgan
Chapter Two: Love at First Sight

August 1, 2005 was just a normal day at Sunset Beach. We woke up at about 9:30 a.m. to the smell of breakfast. My mom always makes breakfast for our house of twelve people. (I mean eight people. The house is only allowed that many.) We had the most delicious scrambled eggs and bacon, but of course, it tasted the same each day.

We stay on Sunset Beach in North Carolina; on 29th street at the house named "Summerville." Even though we reside there, we go to the beach on the other side of the island on 16th street. So that morning we got everyone up, ready, and loaded up the car with chairs, coolers, sand tools, sports equipment, towels, etc. By the time we actually got to the beach it was about 11:30 a.m. When we stepped off the pier-bridge, all we saw was our huge semi circle. The semi circle of people was smaller than usual; probably about ten out of the thirty were missing. I didn't think much of it. I just figured they were on their way.

So I just sat there and read for about an hour, waiting for my clan to show up. Mary and Sara were the only people I ever wanted to hang out with. After about an hour, I decided to ask someone where they were, "They're not coming today," someone responded. I can still hear those terrible words in my head. It always sucks when they don't come. I have to actually hang out with other people in my family that I would prefer not to spend time with.

It was so hot and I was tired of reading. I decided to go into the water for a while. I walked in slowly as the small calm waves slapped against my legs. The water was warm but refreshing. It was exactly what I needed to cool off my burning skin. As I was walking I saw this huge circular yellow raft. It looked like it could fit about twenty people in it. It looked like so much fun. Needless to say, it was definitely the talk of the beach. Everyone was jealous.

I finally got out to where everyone was after about five minutes of trucking out into the ocean. I was the just awkwardly standing there alone. But not for long. Here comes Kyle! Now Kyle is my grandfather's best friend's grandson. I know, yes I am one of those people who explain things like that in a circular way. At this point he was in 8ᵗʰ grade and just discovering girls and he chose me as his little experiment. He is just one of those people that get under your skin and shatters your tolerance.

So Kyle came over to me and had his "A" game on! He was "flirting" and everything and he tried to get with me. Of course I was trying to get away! I started to float on my back away from him. His four-foot tall self came running after me and scooped me up like a baby. He continued to talk to me, and then attempted to lay one on me. I freaked out and ran away to my friend Scotty, to protect me. I was so traumatized that I made Scotty and his friend Jon not leave my side for the rest of the day.

There I was, frantically hiding from another deadly kiss. My eyes started to wander the ocean. And then I saw them. Out of all the people on that beach, I saw these two guys about 200 feet away. One of them was pretty tall, about six feet. He was really tan, and had a pretty nice body and a short buzz cut. The other was average height; probably about five feet seven inches tall. He was leaning towards the pale side with dark semi-shaggy hair. I wanted to know them. For some reason, something was luring me to them. I wanted to talk to them. I planned on going over and meeting them. Before I got the chance, probably 20 people in a huge group surrounded them. I missed my chance.

Now I never believed in love at first sight before that day. I will always remember what I thought the first time I saw them. "Those guys are going to change mine and Mary's life forever." I had never met them, never even seen them and that's what I was thinking? I know it sounds crazy and ridiculous but that's the truth. It was around three or four o'clock and it was time to leave. My goal was left undone. I had failed. I didn't meet them. I felt so much regret it wasn't even funny. "I'll never see them again. What if they really were supposed to change me? Did they notice me? I missed my chance." My mind was going crazy and I didn't know what to do. All this from two guys I'd never even met before.

Via Mary
Tuesday, Day 1
Chapter Three: The Mystery Guy

Waking up this morning, I had no idea of the magnitude of this day. You see I'd like to believe that every love story has a unique and distinct beginning; you can rest assured knowing that this story is no different. It begins with the number eight, an upright infinity symbol, which would have never had any significance if it hadn't been the month in which I met him. The one who would inevitably change my life and show me sides of myself that perhaps would have never come to be without him.

There we were in the ocean, it was the normal group of girls, just the three of us: Morgan, Sara, and I. There were also the usual guys: Scotty, Jon, and Kyle. We were all hanging out joking around about the latest mishap that one of us had. The vacation was still young if you will; it was the first day that we were actually all together, so there really wasn't anyone to make fun of, yet. So naturally the focus was making fun the people on the beach around us. Usually I didn't like to take part in the shallow judgment of strangers, but with the ripe feeling of resentment for Brandon, I indulged myself. It probably wasn't the most mature thing to do, but we were shallow teenage girls with a lot of growing up to do. For some of us it would come soon, really soon, like in-the-next-couple-of-days soon.

The sun was intense but we couldn't really feel it because the waves were too busy beating the crap out of us. Looking back at the shore, we could see the circle of chairs where our parents would sit, talking and drinking…a lot. We watched the boys toss the football, and of course picking on RJ, oh how angry Morgan and I would get at them for that. We watched Ashley cling to maturity by promptly ditching us to hang out with Amy and Becky. Don't get me wrong, I have nothing against them, in fact I rather admire them, its just, if I am going to come to the ocean I'm not going to spend the majority of my time sitting in a chair looking at it. I'm going to be in the water from the time I get there until I have to leave. Coming out of the water for us was rare, usually only to eat and grab the occasional bottle of water.

For me, being in the ocean was more than just a time to hang out with friends and relax, my whole life I have always loved being in the water, not necessarily swimming but just being. I can't explain what I felt with the ocean, we had this kinship—a mutual understanding of each other. I would allow it to pull me out to where I could barely touch, always knowing that it would bring me back safely. To put it lightly, I was mesmerized by the waves. The way they would gently lift my body up and then place me back down, gave me peace. When I was out jumping waves no one else existed. I was allowed to be a part of something so much bigger than myself, and I got lost in it.

Snapping back to reality, I realized Morgan and Sara were calling our most favorite person ever! Yes you guessed it, it was Kyle! Now, how do I go about explaining Kyle without over doing it towards any extreme? Kyle's a good kid, with good intentions; it's just that sometimes his energy outweighs his communication skills, rendering him annoying instead of friendly. However, I do believe he is a great person; he just needs to remember to stop and take it down a notch. So I looked over to see what Kyle was doing this time and what do you know! He was talking to and clearly annoying some other guy who was not a part of our herd. When I saw the look on the mystery guy's face I promptly swam over and grabbed Kyle providing ample apologies for his "friendliness." The mystery guy was cute up close, although my face was a wee bit sunburned, I know I was probably blushing too. He was tall, I'd say about 6'0 at the time, he was very tan, he had short dark hair, not quite a buzz cut but close enough to it. Man I looked stupid and probably borderline crazy as I dragged Kyle back over to Morgan and Sara who were not thrilled in the least to have him back in the herd, I looked back over at the mystery guy, did I mention how cute he was? To my disappointment he was busy with his boogey board trying to catch waves. Morgan and Sara being the darling friends that they were noticed just how taken I was with the mystery boy that they wasted no time before making fun of me. How could I be that drawn to him? I didn't even know his name! In attempt to get away from the two jokesters, I decided I was hungry and it was definitely time for lunch.

Now I've never been one for timing but I have to say, looking back on this, even I was impressed with myself. As I walked out to get lunch, I realized I was going to pass the mystery guy so I quickly decided that this would be my chance to formally introduce myself. Just as I was making eye contact, ready to say hello, a huge wave knocked me off balance and into the ocean to which the mystery guy promptly replied with, "There's a wave there." In that moment I wasn't sure if I should curse Mother Nature or just drown myself on the spot. Both of those seemed a little extreme so I followed my ultra-cool girl instinct (yeah right I had no game!) and replied with an oh so smooth, "Yeah, thanks." Then proceeded to swim as fast as I could back to shore. Man I was such an idiot!

Walking up to the cooler, I replayed the whole situation in my head, yeah definitely not what I was going for. If he didn't think I was a complete crazy person when I had to drag Kyle away, my little collision with the wave was sure to keep him from ever wanting to know me, right? As I was eating my super awesome double stacker PBJ, I caught myself looking for him in the ocean. What was I doing? How pathetic could I possibly be? I milled over the situation a little while longer and then decided to get back in the water, this time armed with a boogey board of my own. Before I could reach Sara and Morgan I heard this guy's voice— the voice I would come to know so well.

He said, "Hi, I'm Victor, I'm half Cuban and no I didn't float over to the US on a cardboard box." In case you were wondering, yes that's when I knew that he would be someone I would know all of my life. With a cautious laugh I began that rest of my life by answering,

"Hi, I'm Mary, and I really am sorry about earlier!"

"It's not a problem, he wasn't really bothering me," and then he motioned toward the boogie board floating lazily in my hands, "Do you boogie board?"

A little wary about my skills being rusty, I answered with a quick yes and then did what any fun loving teenage girl would do... "Hey Victor, I challenge you to a wave riding competition!"

"Alright, you're on!" He replied curtly, man his eyes were a dazzling blue.

"Great first one to catch ten waves wins." I said, hoping my eyes shined half as brightly as his.

The next half hour or so consisted of me kicking Victor's butt and me gently reminding him of the score and who was winning—yeah that's right it was I. He mostly complained that I was smaller so the waves could carry me further, bullshit if you ask me. By the time it was over, we had been laughing and talking as if we hadn't just met thirty minutes ago. Did I mention I kicked his butt ten to three? Although the victory was great, there was something even better than that. The conversations we were having, in retrospect, blew me away. We kept talking about random things for example I found out he was my age (fifteen at the time), he lives in Florida, played soccer, wrestled, has two sisters (one older and one younger), and most importantly, he believed in God. Even then I found myself utterly impressed by the situation. How often can two complete strangers come together without flirting mind you and just have a legitimate conversation without a hint of ulterior motives? By that point, I had no doubt in my mind that this guy would be very hard to forget.

Being that I was still a fifteen-year-old girl, the most important thing at the time was yet to be revealed: did my best friends Sara and Morgan actually like this Victor guy, or was I just captivated by the illusion of what I perceived to be an amazing person? To my relief, my two hypercritical best friends actually liked him. With that question resolved, I began to believe that maybe by some crazy slim chance, this could actually turn out to be something real. As the day wore on, time tricked us into thinking it had stopped when really it was flying by. So much so that when Victor's younger sister CeCe came over to get him because his grandmother wanted them home, it felt like only ten minutes had passed. (Apparently it was three hours, I still have my doubts.) Before he left he asked if I would be here tomorrow, so I quickly told him I'd be here all week. He smiled and said he'd see me then.

That night, back at the house with Sara and our families, I could barely concentrate on my dinner. Victor was always on my mind. I didn't usually like guys like this, especially not this fast. I couldn't understand why I was so taken with him; he was just a guy, what was the big deal? But, there was just something about him, about our time together that made this seem bigger than what it was, bigger than us. I couldn't shake the thought of him from my mind. I didn't understand this wasn't how this was supposed to be, I was supposed to be cool and confident, yet I was obsessing over every word, and every detail of our time together. Again it begged the question, what was the big deal?

I must say, one of the benefits of living with eight people in a house designed for six is that you get to share rooms. For Sara and I, this meant girl talk until we fell asleep, and the hot topic for tonight: Victor. I found myself in a peculiar situation because I've always been the girl who gets pretty much whatever she wants. I was always the one being chased, never the chaser, so this Victor kid really had me thrown for a loop. Sure he was tall, dark, and handsome but I was petite, cute, and funny and the more I thought about it the more I doubted he wasted his night thinking of me. Regardless, I was intrigued, and that night was one Sara and I spent in analytical girl mode. I went to bed that night at ease yet discontented because although I've had my fair amount of relationships (as many as a fifteen-year-old girl can have) they had a knack for ending in disaster, and I pleaded with God to make this one different. The fact that I live to write this should be proof enough that the big man upstairs is pretty good at his job. So after talking Sara into oblivion I decided she was allowed to go to bed, and I followed shortly after. Usually when I sleep in a new place for a while I can't get to sleep right away, but that night, I slept better than ever and I can't help but think that it was because of him.

Via Morgan
Chapter Four: And We Meet

Another day passes. It is Tuesday. The day starts the same way: eggs, bacon, and this time, sausage. Actually it was only the same because of the breakfast. My grandma said she wanted to go shopping. Of course I go with them! I mean what teenage girl would turn down shopping? We decided to go to Myrtle Beach. We went to the normal stores we go to every year, but of course nothing changed about them. We went to places like the Curious Mermaid, Mole Hole, Victoria's Rag Patch, and Island Breeze.

By the time we got to the beach it was about one o'clock in the afternoon. As I roamed the semi circle to complete the trio (and yes I am just going to call us all different things each time.) I bragged about all my purchases. Bragging has become like a tradition and a necessity with us. After about five minutes of searching and bragging I find them. I was so excited to see them. I hadn't seen them in two days and there was a lot to talk about. I mean we had to talk about everything from my totally cute new Vera Bradley to the incident with Kyle. I'm not going to lie I was overly excited.

Something was different though. They were with someone I didn't know, a boy. I'm not exactly sure how they met him, but there he was. Mary had her game on with him. They were flirting and a blind person could see the chemistry. After about fifteen minutes, I realized who he was. He was the tall, tan one from the day before. I was stunned. His name was Victor. Finally I had a name to the face. Victor was a fifteen-year-old half Cuban from Florida. The trio and Victor sat and laughed for about a half hour. I couldn't help but wonder about the other kid. Would he come around?

My brother RJ loves the ocean but he hates crabs, fish, shells, and water deeper than his belly button. He balances this by always being on a boogie board, so his feet cannot touch the ground. Needless to say the current pulls him out a lot. That's what happened on this day. The current pulled him out about a block down the beach. He was alone, and scared. He was screaming at the top of his lungs. I saw him and I went running I just hate it when he's upset. I finally got to him and pulled him back with me and pleaded with him to put his feet down. I was almost completely back when I looked up. There he was right in front of me, guy number two. He was the pale one with black shaggy hair. He was a lot cuter up close. He had the cutest little half mustache.

So as I said, I looked up and he was there. Well, that's true but I was literally right next to him. I was pulling the boogie board so I was leaning over. I'm sure he was staring at my chest but I don't blame him. I had huge tatas back then. Anyway I perked up and introduced myself. Sometimes I like to look at it like he must have seen it. Here's some chick bending over, huge boobs in your face. I probably came off as a slut. Mary and Sara make fun of me saying I squeezed my arms together when I introduced myself. No wonder he talked to me.

His name was Zack. At the time he was fourteen years old. He lived in Pittsburgh, Pennsylvania. He played football, basketball, baseball, and was a huge Steelers' fan. He was fun and different than what I was used to. We had some stuff in common, but we had a lot of things that contradicted each other. We fought a lot. We had a connection right off the bat.

For a while it was just Mary, Sara, Victor, Zack, and I just talking and getting to know each other. The first time Mary and I were alone I asked her, "Which one do you want?"

27

Her response was, "Victor."

"Shit. Oh well I've always wanted to hook up with someone with a mustache." I can't lie I was ridiculous back then.

It had started.

Mary and I spent every possible moment with them. We'd be in a huge group with all of our friends and all of theirs, but honestly I don't remember ever seeing them. I only remember seeing Zack, Mary, and Victor. It was like at that moment nothing else mattered, probably because it didn't.

For the first time in my life I felt comfortable with him. I had only known him for a few hours and I trusted him. I was completely willing to open myself up to him. I could tell he was genuine, sweet, and completely innocent. I have always had issues with trusting people, but for some reason, it was so easy to trust him.

That first day Zack and I spent about three hours talking. I couldn't even tell you what about because I have no clue. All I remember is that I came out of that day feeling different somehow. I had never connected with someone so fast before. Trust me that scared the crap out of me. I tried so hard to deny it, but after just a few hours, I had already started to have feelings for him. The scariest part was definitely that I didn't know if I would ever see him again. Also, what if he didn't want to hang out me again tomorrow? All these emotions and more just lead me up to feel very, very dumb. I hated liking him so early. Actually, I hated liking him at all. It made me vulnerable.

When I got home, I spent an hour or so just standing on our balcony. Just looking at the ocean in the distance. I didn't know what to do. I didn't know what to feel. I thought about Zack, the ocean, Mary, and Jeff. What was I going to tell him? I decided I wouldn't tell him quite yet. I just wanted to figure out what to say to him so he wouldn't freak out.

"Jesus Christ, Morgan! What are you doing? You have to be ready in an HOUR!" My father has always been such a kind man. I hope you can tell my sarcasm.

That night was Oscar's night. One night a year we go to Oscar's; it's just a simple Steelers bar, but it's a tradition. All thirty of us go have the times of our lives. It's everyone's favorite night by far. It was different that year though. Mary and I were in our own little worlds. We were both deep in thought and being extremely anti-social. Several times during the night people came up to me and asked me what was wrong. What they didn't understand was that for once, everything was right in my world. I was starting to be happy for the first time in a long time.

There is one thing I will never forget from that night. I remember going up to my mom and Mrs. Nancy and asking, "How far away is Pittsburgh?"

"Oh! I know why you're asking! You have a thing for that boy. Sorry sweetheart but it's about five hours away."

Damn. They caught me. They knew I liked him. The more important thing was five hours away from my house! Five hours would not work for teenagers! This was just one more reason to be skeptical and feel stupid. No matter what those feelings were that night, I wanted to spend more time with him. I couldn't wait to see Zack's smile. He always just seemed to light up. Believe me, I did too. I was going to make the best of the time we had. I knew that if things worked out right, I could have four whole days, and that would be enough. I had to find a way to make it enough. I wanted it to be a week that I would never forget.

So far I'm sure you've noticed differences in Mary's and my stories. We have discovered that our stories contradict each other at times. I have to admit this is one of the hardest things I have to deal with. Basically what we're saying is our story that came from our memory, and it's everything that we hold dear to our hearts. However you start to second-guess yourself about everything else, until finally you can't tell what's real and what is made up. And then what do you have? Nothing.

Via Mary
Wednesday, Day 2
Chapter Five: Soul Searching

I woke up the next morning and began to re-hash what happened the day before as I lazily stirred my froot loops in the same bowl that I have used since I was three. Being a creature of habit, I had the same routine for the past 12 years and it went a little something like this. Every morning I would come out in my pajamas and sit at our island between the kitchen and the living room, and eat whatever cereal I was into that year, this year like I said, it was froot loops. Usually I'm the last one up, but for whatever reason, I found myself up, and eating alone.

The other important detail you should know about my house is, in the back, there is a big open porch / deck that overlooks a pond seeing as our house is positioned on the tenth hole of a golf course. This porch bears much significance because it's where I did most of my thinking. It's the first place I went the summer after my grandfather passed away. And how hard it was to return to the place that the single most important man in my life had gotten specifically for me. My heart ached to know that he would never again grace the halls that seemed to dim themselves in his absence. He would never add more golf balls to his collection that hung with much pride on the wall in the living room. Though I was twelve at the time, I could sense the irrevocable gloom that seemed to sink into the carpets and the walls. The magnitude of the situation hit me hard as I lazily rocked back and forth, the first summer without my grandfather. Even though we only ever shared the house with him in person once, his absence felt heavy, I felt heavy at the realization of the permanence of the situation. This morning I decided would be no different then every other lazy summer day. So after I trekked around the island to put my bowl in the sink, I went to sit on the porch, however I was feeling kind of lonely so I grabbed some bread and sat by the edge of the pond and fed the snapping turtles. As they happily clicked their jaws, I noticed something: for the first time in years, I felt content. You see, ever since my grandfather passed away and my Aunt Susan the year after him, I went through a deep depression for two years and ever since then no matter what I did to deal with it I felt a deep incongruity within myself. My heart, though recently mended and quite delicate, told me I was missing something. Often times I would fill these gaps with meaningless relationships sprinkled with a touch of broken promises and general apathy. My grandfather and aunt were two of the most important and influential people in my life and at the same time I thought I was supposed to replace them. But I quickly realized that it couldn't be done. I became more and more pathetic as I would throw myself into relationships for the sake of trying to feel some type of human emotion.

Needless to say this first day with Victor really shook me up because I was just getting over some other worthless relationship and had sworn off guys. But God had other plans. To this day, over four years later, I still can't tell you why this guy just so happened to be different, or how I knew because I still don't know. For all I know, there may have never been a second day, or any other day for that matter. But for whatever reason, the days would go on, and surely enough he was in them. That morning I felt content, and in my heart of hearts, I knew it was because of Victor, and for the first time in a long time, I was okay with that. So I sat there in my green rocking chair and let the sweet South Carolina morning take me away—and so it did. And as if they choreographed it, one by one, the rest of my family began to wake up and I could hear life restored once again in the Bosley household. I remained outside though I could hear the chatter over who got the remote and the desperate desire to know what it was that everyone wanted for breakfast. So much for a calm South Carolina morning! But I was more than glad to be greeted by Sara dressed in her matching pajamas though her hair was a bit disheveled.

"Hey, Cuban lover." She greeted me, oh so fondly.

"Morning sunshine." I replied, ignoring her snarky greeting.

"So I bet someone is excited to go to the beach this afternoon," she said continuing to mock my apparent infatuation.

"Yeah it should be fun times, did the parentals decide on when we are heading over yet?" I asked, trying to remain cool and calm although my stomach was doing flips that Olympians would envy.

"Yeah I think some time around 11:30," she said, either ignoring my excitement or just generally not caring. That was Sara though, always a morning person.

And with that, I got up and went into my room to pick out the cutest bathing suit I could find and proceed to stare at myself in the mirror, try another three bathing suits on repeat the analysis, and eventually end up wearing the first one I tried on. Oh the joys of being a teenage girl! As I walked into the hallway I could hear the chaos of loading food and drinks into coolers, towels and sunscreen into bags, and kids and boogie boards into cars. When we finally were all loaded up and ready to go the nervous anticipation began. So many thoughts and questions went through my head. Would he be there? Would he come up to me or would I have to go up to him? What if he isn't there at all? Needless to say the car ride was torture.

As I sit here debating my diction and syntactical structure, I can't help but smile lovingly at the second day I spent with Victor. When I walked towards the familiar semi-circle of the same faded beach chairs from the years before. I remember dropping everything, failing to put on sunscreen, and just looking for him. As soon as I saw him I got painstakingly nervous. For someone who grew up with their only sibling being their older brother and all of his friends, I was ridiculously bad at talking to guys. But I swallowed my nerves and told myself to be cool—fat chance!

"Well look at who it is!" he said, and yes, his eyes were still a dazzling blue.

"Hey Victor, what's up?" [STUPID ALERT]

"Eh not much what about…"

"And what are you two doing?" Sara and Morgan called out in unison.

I would have been mad but I was drowning in my own nervousness so I welcomed their diversion with open arms.

"Victor, you remember Sara and Morgan from yesterday, right?"

"Yeah, sup guys?" he said with a coolness in his tone that I only wish I could conjure.

They mumbled some ambiguous response and then I noticed a new face heading our way, which apparently wasn't so new seeing as Victor and Morgan were quick to greet this "Zack" character. He was of a medium height, maybe 5'7 at the time; he had dark brown medium-length hair, you know, not quite shaggy-surfer-dude style, but not quite clean-cut either. He also had what we would later deem a half-mustache. No, he didn't shave one half and leave the other; it was just very thin so us girls called it a "half mustache." He had a boyish handsomeness to him, and he wore a faded Steelers hat into the ocean, weird. (The famous rhetorical question whenever we got into a play fight would be, "Who wears hats in the ocean?") I remember the hat simply because you could tell it was originally white but had turned yellow due to sweat and the salt water, I would assume. Luckily he was good at taking jokes because by the end of the trip many would be coming his way. He had a friendly look to him, you know one of those people that you immediately feel comfortable around whether or not you knew him all your life or for just a few seconds.

However the first thing I noticed were Morgan's huge smile and a hint of blushing upon greeting Zack. Before we came to the beach, Morgan had been in her first serious relationship, seriously abusive. From the moment our family members met him we knew he was no good. I mean, from the way he acted blatantly sexual with her right in front of us, to his thuggish attire, we knew it had to be ended. Sara, Ashley and I made it our mission to pull the wool from her eyes, and it took many months. He never hit her but he definitely controlled her every move and mood. So when we went down we had the full intention of making a girl's trip because I had just closed a two-year wound if you will. I specifically remember the car ride down listening to "The Best I'll Ever Be" by Sister Hazel and thinking about my ex. Who knew that I would be listening to the exact same song on the way back, thinking of someone completely different? In any event Morgan smiled in a way that I hadn't seen in months, and that's when I knew with 100 percent certainty that these two boys would change our lives, for good.

After greeting Zack, Morgan pulled me aside and said in her very Morgan, "Which one do you want?"

I replied with a quick, "Victor of course!"

For whatever reason, she looked momentarily disappointed but, a huge smile broke out across her face and with a quick "Okay" from her, we rushed back over to the guys pretending that we weren't just talking about them.

Zack fit so easily into our group, as did Victor; it was as if they were supposed to be there all along. Growing up, that's what I had always heard too: when you find the one you're supposed to be with, it will be easy. Though there will be hard times for the most part it will be easy, natural even. This realization, of course, is in retrospect, as I was too busy trying to get Victor's apparently sparse attention. He was distant today, which was weird, not in a rude way either, he just seemed like he had his mind on other things. Being the insecure fifteen-year-old girl that I was, that immediately set off an endless litany of questions in my head. Was I making all of this up? Did he really not feel the same way as I did?

He got out of the water frequently and one of the times he went to play soccer with his sister Cece. I couldn't help but think it was the cutest thing ever. My brother and I didn't exactly have the closest relationship back then so to see two siblings hanging out like that, it really warmed my heart. I guess the other thing was I knew that he was the older sibling so I thought it was super cute that he took the time to play with his younger sister. Not that she was that much younger, based on her looks she looked about a year or two younger. In any event seeing him play soccer with Cece was adorable and I was okay that he took a break from me to pay attention to her. He eventually warmed up later in the day and everything seemed to be back to normal. As if we actually had a normal, this was just the second day of me knowing him. Our herd seemed to take a natural divide because unfortunately for Sara there was no third dream guy waiting to sweep her off her feet so as Zack, Victor, Morgan, and I got closer, Sara hung back with Ashley, though occasionally hanging out with us too. We stayed in the water for hours, never daring to come out, in case this was actually all a dream and if we got out of the water then all of this would somehow disappear. The four of us seemed so natural together, our lives just blending in with one another.

It wasn't long before our conversations wandered and it was all about the jokes. It was one of the times that Sara felt like hanging out with us, and so we fell swiftly back into our usual routine: making fun of random strangers. Sara was either eager to impress us, or just incredibly outgoing so she started it off.

35

"Look at that lady over there, she's just like Zack wearing a hat in the ocean, who even does that?" Sara said in a snide tone. To which all of us started to laugh, except for Zack.

"Uh Sara, that's my mom" Zack said. This should have made things awkward but instead we all just kind of laughed harder.

Sara replied with a quick "Oh" and mumbled an apology and we continued to talk about random things. It was so easy to get to know the boys; they were so open and kind hearted. Eventually as the conversation grew more intense, Sara seemed to back off and go hang out with other parts of the herd. I'm not sure how long it was that we talked but sooner than we knew, Cece came over to claim Victor. With a sigh and quick goodbye with a promise of there being a tomorrow, he was gone.

Zack and Morgan were off somewhere doing only God knows what so I went to try and find Sara in attempt to make up on some of our lost girl time. When I found her, I could tell she was glad to have me back. Growing up, Sara and I were never particularly close. Her personality was always fickle and I was quite the ornery child so we often clashed. Trust me Sara even has journal entries from when we were little that say things like "Mary is just jealous of me" or "Erik (my brother) is my favorite cousin." We, in short, just never saw eye to eye. However now that we are older we're pretty much inseparable. I love Sara so much; she is one of the only people, who supported me when things took a turn for the worst. You know, it's easy to cherish things once you lose them, but it's exceptionally rare to appreciate them while you have them. So for having Sara in my life, let it be known that I am forever grateful.

Sara and I mostly just hung out in the water, jumping waves, and shooting the breeze. I made sure not to talk about Victor only because I wanted this time that we spent together to be about us and not about him. Besides I had just met him and it was absurd for me to have the feelings that I had for him. And if she wanted to talk about him then I knew that she would bring him up though I wasn't expecting her to at all. I guess the other thing you should know is that I am extremely protective of my family and I never ever want to see them in pain or even just annoy them because I love them so much. So I kind of have a tendency to baby people, which really is a problem. Sara took this little personality quirk in stride. As much as I didn't want to talk about Victor, I really, really did want to talk about him. I could talk about him all day if someone were dumb enough to care and actually let me go on that long.

Before we cared enough to realize that the sun was setting, our parents called us from the water, as it was time to go home. Tonight was going to be a good night simply because tonight was our favorite night: Oscar's night. Oscar's is a little bar / restaurant that our entire herd goes to for dinner once every year. Let me just tell you, it's the most amazing night ever. Although the food isn't what I would call amazing, the fact that our entire group gets to sit down for a meal is what always makes my day. But as I would soon come to discover, this year would be different. (Last year was my punk / emo phase.) This year I would be so love struck that I wouldn't be the social butterfly that my family was used to having around. And that is exactly what they noticed. If I remember correctly Morgan was the same way too, quiet and lost in her little world, which I assumed had Zack in it as well. We couldn't help ourselves; we were drawn to these boys for reasons that, quite frankly, were beyond us. It's funny because you would think that we would at least talk to each other about this whole situation. However this was beyond words, it was beyond us. The power of the situation left us at a loss for words. So we spent that night secluded by an invisible bond that neither of us could even fathom.

When we got back to the house, my mind as it lately did, drifted back to Victor. At this point I was pretty much praying that he was thinking about me too. It was almost as if I willed it to happen. It was even nice to have someone to think about at the end of the day. Although I'd been in a wealth of relationships, never did I actually take the time to really learn to care about them. All I can say is that in the equivalent of two days I had seemed to grow a few years emotionally. That night, as I lay restlessly in bed it hit me.

Could I really grow to love him or had I already reached that point?

Via Morgan
Chapter Six: The Test

I woke up Wednesday morning with butterflies already in my stomach. What would happen today? Would I see him? I lay in bed just trying to forget about him, collect myself, and be able to pretend my life was the same as it was three days earlier. It took about thirty minutes to compose myself.

Downstairs, it sounded like there was a party. It was 9:30 in the morning and these people were screaming, fighting, and laughing. I had to see what was going on. Plus the bacon was calling my name. Damn! I was hungry! I walked down the steps and all I saw was Jorge (GW, my grandfather's best friend.) I knew it was trouble right then and there. I sat down, made a plate, and started to eat.

"Hey Morgan! I have a really good story for you. I had a triple flusher this morning! "

"Oh God. Do I want to know?" he nods. "Okay, fine tell me. What is a triple flusher?"

"I had to take a shit this morning. So I go in and I was in there for 20 minutes. I stunk up the whole house. I mean this shit hurt. I was so big I had to flush three times before it actually went down!" The man went into graphic detail about his poop! Now here I am sitting at the table just trying to eat my bacon, and he is talking about poop! I was beyond grossed out. But yet, at the same time he helped calm my nerves. Thank God for poop! Wow! Did I really just say that?

Everyone was basically awake by this point, everyone except for my sister. She was passed out in the couch. An earthquake couldn't wake her up. She had been on the phone with her latest boyfriend till about 5:00 a.m., and it was now 10:00 a.m. She has been known for not being able to show life until having at least eight hours of sleep. We tried for about an hour to wake her up but she just wasn't having that. Finally we just left her at home. We got to the beach at about 11:00 am.

The first thing I did was run and get Mary. She was pretty close so it wasn't hard. Today we didn't fool around; we went right into the water. We did not talk to anyone; we didn't even put on sunscreen. Just as soon as we saw each other we started walking into the water.

For some reason we didn't go straight into the water. We kind of made a detour. I don't know if there was a game of football right ahead but we didn't go straight. We went a bit further down the beach. There he was. He was building a sandcastle with some little kids. What a loser! I smiled at him and just kept walking. About a minute later, while our backs are already turned to him, I heard him yell, "You guys going into the ocean?"

I turned my head wondering and hoping he was talking to us. He was! A permanent smile was on my face. "Yeah come on in with us," I said, holding my breath just desperately hoping he would take me up on my offer. I just needed him to want to spend the day in the ocean with me.

Right away he started to get up. Of course, we didn't wait for him, but he looked so eager to come be with us. Well I hoped just me. I wish I could remember why we didn't go straight in. His family was not right next to us either. He was probably like two or three people down the beach. Honestly, if we didn't take that detour I don't know if I would have ever seen him again. Fate works in mysterious ways, and I love it.

Mary and I finally reached our spot in the ocean. We sat there for a minute or two trying to figure out what would happen that day. I was trying to figure out what I wanted, who I wanted. Then I realized, what I wanted was tearing through the waves trying to get to me. But, was I what he wanted?

His eyes weren't a good enough answer. Looking back, I don't know how I could have second-guessed it. His eyes showed passion, desire, and emotion. They were like nothing I had ever seen before. No one had ever looked at me that way. I'm nothing special. I'm not a skinny girl. I have curves. I have a huge red birthmark spreading down my entire left leg. Like my cousin once told me, "No one will ever want to be with you." Despite all of that, Zack looked at me like I was the only person he could see. He looked at me like I was something worthwhile. I was something special, and for a second I actually believed what his eyes were telling me.

I had to test him, though. I needed to know for sure what he thought, so I put him through little situation to see how he would react and then I would know how he felt. I know, I am just that brilliant. Okay, I am just that insecure. So while we were in a big group and there were a lot of distractions, I slipped away. I swam about 100 feet away to where I could almost not touch the bottom. I just sat there watching the waves crash all the way into the horizon. There I stood, shaking, wondering how long it would take my prince charming to come rescue me. Was he feeling the same way?

After a minute or two, I heard his voice. I turned around to see his eyes different from what they were five minutes ago. They were filled with worry and maybe even a little sorrow. He was concerned about me. It was a look I had rarely seen. It was a look that I understood right away. He cared about me and wanted me to be happy. Weird right?

"What's wrong? Why are you all the way out here?" he said with great concern for me.

He passed the test. From that moment on, I knew he was interested. I couldn't help but smile. He noticed me. He followed me. He made me feel special. I could feel myself glowing. He made me glow.

So in response to his question, "Nothing. I just had to get away from the commotion; sometimes it's too much for me to handle." It was the perfect cover. I was proud to have thought so quickly on my feet and he bought it too! It started up a conversation and everything. For the first time that whole day, we were alone together. It together was rare, but I cherished every moment of it.

After everyone saw us swim off together, they got the hint that we wanted to be alone. We were alone for a surprisingly long time. It was a lot longer than we had been alone before. The wind started to blow hard. I was freezing. I'm not exactly sure how I was so cold considering it was probably about eighty degrees. I mean it was August in North Carolina. Well I sat down into the water as low as I could get. I sat with the water up to my chin and my hands out of sight. "Are you really that cold?" Zack said meanly.

"Yes I am that cold leave me alone." I snapped back.

We sat there talking for a while. We both just tried to ignore my body convulsions. We were having a lovely conversation probably about football. Just then, we saw Amy and Becky, the two older cool girls. They were coming towards us. I just knew they would try to embarrass me. Amy Rosario has known me since I was in the womb, but had also been my babysitter for about eight years or something ridiculous like that. Needless to say, she had a lot of dirt on me.

She yells "HAND CHECK." I immediately without even thinking threw my hands into the air. Amy, being the experienced adult she was, thought that I was doing inappropriate things below the water. The only issue was that we really weren't even that close to each other. So it really wasn't even that possible for me to be doing that in the first place.

Amy was being overprotective and honestly, kind of a jerk. I mean I love her for it and it really created one of my favorite memories, but it was kind of a jerk move. That was Amy, though. She did everything for the laughs. After that comment she didn't say much else. She had gotten her point across, and now we were slightly terrified at what everyone was thinking that we were doing out there.

Zack and I sat there laughing about it for a few minutes. He had never seen Amy or Becky before so he was a little taken aback at the idea of them yelling at us. I had to explain to him exactly who they were. I just explained that Amy was Scotty's sister and Becky was Amy's best friend.

After a quick recap of their history, we were back into our original conversation. We were talking about our lives and our cites. We talked about just about anything that was unimportant. We were alone again. It was perfect.

After maybe an hour, the ruckus came roaring over to Zack and I. Ashley and Sara came swimming over to us screaming at each other. There had been a vicious game of football. Sara was complaining about Ashley stacking the teams and clothes lining her. Needless to say, they convinced us to play.

We all trucked out of the water to what I expected to be the death of me. Football with the boys and Ashley. Now honestly I was more afraid of Ashley' who stood at a whopping 5'2" and 100 lbs. Rather than my cousin Nick who like 5'11" and 200 lbs. She is vicious! Sara won the argument, though. Everyone felt bad and made the game into a two-hand-touch game. So lame! Everything is better when you can hurt people!

Zack was on my team. We lost miserably, not even going to lie. It was so much fun though. Ashley's team was stacked so we didn't even really have a chance. For a time Zack was the quarterback, and almost every time, he would try to throw it to me. Yet every time, I would drop it. He was mean about it too.

"All you know about football, I expected you to at least be able to catch it." He liked to pick on me probably because I would start picking on him.

After the game, we all separated. It was about time I got something to eat considering I was starving. I went to the semi-circle of chairs and dug into my peanut butter and jelly sandwich with crunchy peanut butter. My mom always says, "You get creamy for home and crunchy at the beach, so you don't know if your eating sand." Anyways, I sat there catching up with my family. I listened to my dad tell his fabulous story about the Mexicans throwing rocks at him because my sister stole the car, making him have to walk to the beach. After about ten minutes I was done with them, after all I could talk to them anytime.

I grabbed Sara and we headed back into the water. There he was all alone, just waiting for us. He had the most disgusting hat on. At one point it had been white but now it was yellow. In addition to the discoloration, it was a Steelers hat...in the ocean? You have to understand that I am from Baltimore, and I am a huge Ravens fan. Ravens and all of Baltimore despise the Steelers. If you ask me why, I couldn't tell you, but that's what you do when you are a Ravens fan. Yeah so this caused lots of problems. I already had feelings for him but I mean this rivalry was a big deal, and kind of a part of me. So what did I do?

I addressed my concern. It became an all-out brawl. It was kind of like two three-year-olds fighting over a Barbie. "No it's mine." Except it was more like, "My team is the best in the league. Your team sucks!" Then we proceeded to spit out some crazy stats like, "The Steelers went 15-1 this year."

"And who was that one, yes that's right, the Ravens! And you owe your season to us because we hurt your quarterback" I like my stats better. It shut him up for a minute. I mean, I'm cute and I actually know what I'm talking about. After about fifteen minutes of the three of us fighting, Sara looked over and saw another lady with a hat on in the ocean and said,

"Hey that lady is weird like you and wears hats in the ocean!"

"Um, that's my mom," states the semi-hurt Zack.

44

So he brought her over and we met her. I would just like to say his mother is by far my favorite person alive, or dead, next to Jesus that is. She is just the sweetest woman I have ever met. After we met her, we had to say goodbye for the day. And what a fabulous day it was. We both agreed that we would see each other tomorrow. I was so excited to see him that next day. When I got home from the beach that day, I ventured right up to the porch again. I don't know why it helps me but it does. Suddenly it dawned on me: I knew exactly what I wanted.

I picked up the phone and called Jeff.

Via Mary
Thursday, Day 3
Chapter Seven: The Adult Play Pen

I woke up in a familiar haze, this time I was back into my routine being the last one up. It was a struggle too! I hated waking up; no amount of food or promises of shopping would do the trick either. I wanted to lie in bed, after all this was vacation. Then I remembered that if I actually did decide to get up it meant I could see Victor. My motivation obviously increased at this realization. I looked over to Sara's bed; the sheets were balled up in the center of it, a familiar sight. Though she wasn't particularly a morning person, she definitely could get up earlier than I did. But then again, so could the dead. I finally willed myself to get up; well that and I had about a dozen people screaming at me to get up. I walked slowly as my legs were still a wee bit wobbly from sleeping and I managed to make it to the island. Without much begging on my end, I got my mom to fix me a bowl of cereal. Froot Loops, the usual.

Around me the usual chaos ensued, packing everything up to get ourselves to the beach. I was still lazily nursing on my froot loops, though I had the adults threatening me to finish or I would be forced to stay behind. I increased my pace and when I was done, it was off to complete the chore of picking out the bathing suit that I would wear. I did the same routine of trying them on and taking them off, of course picking the first one I tried on. You think I would get the hang of this but I was a bit hardheaded and insisted on trying all of them on. With much commentary from the peanut gallery, I made it into the car, and we were off to the beach. The usual nerves kicked in as soon as the car shifted into gear. Thank God for iPods, because if I didn't have music, I think I may have vomited from my nerves. Yeah, it was that bad. Of course, as soon as we got through the back roads there was a huge line for the bridge, ugh f my life! At least when the car was moving, I felt like we were making progress and would be there soon.

After a twenty minute wait for the stupid bridge that I unfortunately love too much to care that it slowed us down, we found ourselves on 16th street, shedding our cover-ups and making a beeline for the water. Of course we were the last ones there, stupid bridge! Morgan, Zack, Victor, Meghan, and Katie were already in the water. So Sara and I got out to them as fast as we could, hoping to spend every second of the rest of the day with them. This day was kind of a blur, but I do have two major memories from them. Allow me to explain.

So there we were, out in the ocean, everyone was just kind of lazily jumping waves, everyone except for Victor and I; we were engaged in really important conversations. We first started talking about which political party we identified with, I won't tell you who were who but I'm sure you can figure it out. We got into different political issues, and what we thought about them. I think the most interesting part of those conversations were that they never turned into arguments, we were truly just talking about how we felt. We gave our opinions on gay marriage, stem-cell research, the death penalty, and abortion. As I said earlier, even if we didn't necessarily agree with each other, it didn't matter; we still talked through the issues. The next big topic of conversation was about Pope John Paul and our feelings about his passing, seeing as he had passed away recently. We both were upset, though we were glad that he wasn't suffering any longer. It was really easy to talk to him because he had a very easy-going personality.

The thing that made the conversations even more fun was the way we were positioned in the water. I was facing the ocean and he was facing the beach. Thinking back on it we probably should have stood sideways but that would've have been as much fun. I say it was fun because during the conversations it was up to me to warn him about the waves. Well I may have "accidentally" forgotten to tell him about a few of them, so when he would get hit with a wave, he would go underwater, grab my legs and flip me. Even though the salt water tasted disgusting when he did it, it was his way of showing me that he liked me and Lord knows I wasn't going to stop that from happening. Overall the day was really enjoyable and both of us definitely had a good time in each other's company. As always though, Cece came up to get Victor, as it was time once again for him to go home to his grandparents. Did I mention that he was up there for a family reunion? Trust me, I felt so bad when I found that out because he was spending the majority of his time with me and not them.

When Victor left, I noticed something very interesting floating in the water. No it wasn't shark or anything but it was a big yellow raft. It looked like it could easily fit a good ten or fifteen people on it. As soon as I saw it, I immediately sought out Morgan to see if she saw it too. I mean this thing was huge, and like I said it looked like tons of fun. I wanted to meet the people with the raft so badly! Morgan, of course, was with Zack at this point so I went over, and in a very excited tone, asked them if they noticed the awesome looking raft. Zack looked over and said, "Yeah it's mine what about it?" My heart soared, I knew the person with that awesome creation!

"Zack can we please please, please go on it, just once, please!?" I practically begged.

"Yeah sure, we'll get a whole group together and go on later." He replied like it was no big deal.

I was thrilled; I was going to get to ride in the big yellow raft. So later that day we got a huge group together to get on the raft it was: Morgan, Zack, Sara, Scotty, Jon, Meghan, Bobby, Katie, and myself from what I remember there may have been more. So we all piled in and what do yah know? It was just as great as I imagined it to be! I mean unless you got stuck facing the ocean as opposed to getting stuck facing the beach. You see, whenever a big wave came up it would hit the raft so hard that the person in the back facing the ocean would get knocked out of the raft. As fun as it was, it was also pretty dangerous because sometimes the raft would go closer to the shore and people could end up stuck under the raft. Luckily, it had a big hole in the middle of it, so some of us managed to go through there when we got stuck under the raft.

The next thing we saw is Aunt Laurie, Morgan's mom, coming out into the ocean towards us. I got really bummed thinking she was coming out to tell us to get out but she had a cooler in her hand. She came up to us and told us that she had popsicles for us, you know the kind that come in the plastic tubes, better known as freeze pops. So once we all had one, she went back to shore, leaving us to get back to our adventure in the raft. There we were, all sitting in the raft, contently eating our freeze pops when a huge wave started to come into shore. Surely enough Morgan and Zack, who were of course sitting next to each other started to head for what I like to call the "ejection seat." The wave crashed into the raft and the next thing we saw is Zack doing a back flip out of the raft freeze pop in hand and everything. We all started to look for him because he didn't come up immediately. Then about ten seconds later we saw a sign of life. Zack's arm shot up with freeze pop in hand and then about another ten seconds later the rest of him came up too. By this time we were laughing so hard because the first thing we saw was just this arm with a freeze pop just hanging out. He got back into the raft and settled in next to Morgan and then he went to take a sip of his freeze pop. Immediately he spit it back out; it was pure salt water, gross!

After the whole freeze-pop ordeal, we went back to enjoying our time on the raft, and laughing at whoever got flipped out. Now apparently, I am credited with "breaking" the raft, and I'd like to clear that little rumor up right now. I, Mary Bosley, did not break the raft, the only thing that I did was notice that there was a small hole in it and when I mentioned it that apparently meant that I broke it. Nevertheless we were really enjoying ourselves, just shooting the breeze. It was so much fun, apparently it was so great that the adults decided that they would come over and kick us out so they could have a turn, thus the official name of the raft became, "the adult play pen."

The day continued with us just hanging out in the water. Eventually the sun began to set and it was time to head homeward bound. And so we did, when we got there my thoughts all went back to him. By this time, I was certain that he had feelings for me, I just didn't know to what extent. I needed to know; I needed to find out somehow. I wasn't about to have someone else ask because I didn't want this to be like middle school all over again but I didn't necessarily have the cajones to ask him myself. So I did what I always do in situations like these: I did nothing. Except think about it a lot, as always I thought myself in circles.

I fell asleep with the realization that tomorrow would be the last day I may ever see him, I had to make this one count.

Via Morgan
Chapter Eight: Popsicles and Play Pens

I woke up the next morning still exhausted. It was not so good of a night. At the same time though, I was excited. The night before, I had called Jeff. I told him about Zack. He could tell that I had feelings for Zack. It was really rough, he yelled at me for about an hour. Now, keep in mind we were technically not dating. I was afraid of what was going to happen when I got home. In my heart I knew that I had done the right thing. It was time for me to be without Jeff. After the tests I knew that I deserved better. I knew that I can be treated better, and I should be. I realized that I needed to be with someone who cares about what I think. I knew that Zack would treat me the way I deserved. Jeff no longer mattered to me. The night before I had decided that everything was over with him. I knew that I would never again crawl back to him. I was better than that now.

I now had nothing to worry about. I had nothing to regret or hold me back. I was really excited; I was ready for Zack to make a move on me. When I got to the beach after our morning ritual, I went straight into the water like I had done the past few days. I found him fairly quickly, considering our families were now best friends. All I had to do was look for the huge group of people. We came together and kind of made our own little circle of friends. It was only a few of us, Megan and Sara. It felt like me and Zack were in our own little world no matter who was around though. No one else mattered. As long as we were together, I was happy.

There I stood, facing him with my back to the waves. At the time I didn't think of it, as a dumb move considering if one little wave came I wouldn't see it and it would crash right into me. I was lost in Zack's eyes. I was still amazed by them and would get lost in them for hours. He was a nice guy and warned me of any bump in the water, I guess he didn't want me to get hurt. One time he turned to me, after the millionth time of warning me and said, "You know, you're the only one I care enough about to warn about the waves." I couldn't breathe. He had just admitted he cared about me. This was monumental for us. It was the perfect thing for him to say. He had placed a permanent smile on my face. However, it totally slipped out of his mouth. He wasn't ready to say that yet or he was afraid I didn't feel the same. Either way, he tried to hide it. He just couldn't stand how forward he had just been. He was really sly and covered it by insulting Megan or something. The effect it had on me had already sank in. Fireworks were exploding in my stomach causing my heart to jump. Oh dear, did he have a hold of my heart!

A little later, I noticed the big yellow raft again. I noticed one new thing about it though: his mom was in it. So I asked him if it was his. It was! I knew the owner of that amazing thing! I made him promise to let me on it just one time, because I wouldn't be able to live with myself if I hadn't missed the opportunity to sit on top the most incredible air-filled creation man kind had ever invented. "Let's just go on now!" offered the man of my dreams.

"No, we don't have to go now. We can go tomorrow or later. I don't care when; I just want to get on eventually." However, my declining was greatly unappreciated by the rest of the crowd. They all wanted to get on it immediately!

We swam over to raft, and one by one swam underneath into the hole directly in the middle. We had to jump super high and have someone pull you up to get on it, because it was about 5 feet high. Plus we were in pretty deep water; needless to say it was difficult. Before I knew it all the kids had kicked the adults off and were having quite a wild and exciting time. We were all having so much fun and ended up being on it for most of the day.

The most important thing to realize about this raft is, it is not meant for the ocean. It's more fun in the ocean, but its just meant for a pool. When waves would come, the person at the back would flip out. I mean you would literally do a back flip out of it. We quickly realized that this would be a fun game that we all wanted to play. I mean a few people ended up getting stuck under there and almost died because of it, but it's all in good fun! I sat next to Zack the whole time and we just talked and had a good time. I remember a few times I fell off the back and he tried to grab my hand to pull me back in. It never worked, but at least he tried. Each and every time he tried to pull me in I saw the same face of concern on his face that I had seen the day before when I tested him. It was something I never would have seen on Jeff. Zack was amazing.

It was the hottest day of the whole week and my mom went to the store and got those freeze pops because the adults couldn't handle the heat with just their alcohol to refresh them. She walked out to the "adult play pen" and gave each of us a popsicle. I guess she thought we were hungry considering we hadn't been out of the water all day, not even for lunch. We were all having a good time eating out popsicles when the "adult play pen" started to turn. Zack and I were heading for the back. Then a huge wave came rushing towards us. We knew that someone was going to flip. That person was Zack.

He did a back flip worthy of a 9.65 in gymnastics out of the raft into the water with his popsicle in hand. He was under for a long time and I was starting to get worried as to where he went. I was worried he was stuck under the boat and couldn't get back out. What if he didn't come up? Finally my fears were put to rest; he was fine. I saw life. No, I didn't see his head pop up gasping for air. No that was too logical for this young Steelers fan. (Steelers fans are usually not the smartest people. So it wasn't something that surprised me much.) I just saw an arm shoot up into the air with a popsicle in the hand trying to save it from the salt water. It was probably another thirty seconds before his head finally came up. He handed me the popsicle while he got back in. Nothing could be heard except explosive laughter. He was really embarrassed. He got himself situated and then proceeded to take a sip of the popsicle. He spit it right out. It was all salt water.

When I think of that week that is the first thing that comes to my mind. Why, I am not so sure, but for some reason it seems to be my favorite memory. Before I left that day, I went to my bag and got out a piece of paper. I wrote down my number, and I gave it to him. I wondered if he would use it. At that point I wasn't even sure if he had anything remotely resembling the feelings I had for him. I was handing him my heart, looking for his face to show me his answer. It was blank. It had no emotion and it killed every single sense of hope in him I had. I'm not sure what I expected maybe jumping for joy, but I got an, "Oh right, okay." So I walked away to hide my wound. I just thought I left Jeff for someone that wasn't interested in me. I thought I was just turned down. I was positive he wasn't interested in me, and I felt part of my heart break right there on that beach. I thought that I would be going home with no one to no one.

Mary and I walked out together. Victor was in front of us. I was complaining about how I hated guys and I was going to stop liking guys altogether. All of this because I didn't think he felt the same way. Mary ignored me, like she had been accustomed to doing when I got like that. However, Victor was intrigued and concerned.

"What about Zack? What happened to him?" He asked

"He doesn't like me, I just know it. And even if he did he won't make a move on me! I just don't understand!" I remarked

"Don't worry; I'll talk to him about it tomorrow." He said.

I didn't think he actually would, but I was very grateful. I was curious and I wanted a secret detective.

Later that night on the way to poker night, I got a text message. It was nothing out of the ordinary. It was pretty dumb, but it made me so incredibly happy. Zack actually texted me. I thought to myself, yes maybe I made the right choice. Maybe I wont end up alone.

Via Mary
Friday, Day 4
Chapter Nine: Four Seashells

This morning I woke up with the knowledge that today would be the last day that I may never be able to stare into those crystal blue eyes again. Today may be the last day that I could see his smile, hear his laugh, and be held in his arms. Today needed to count more than any other day in my life. I needed to know that after today, there would be a tomorrow, and more importantly, I needed to know that he would be in that tomorrow, and every other day to come. I knew waking up this morning that I was undoubtedly in love with him. It only took four days, but I was more certain than ever that this was real. So I started the day the same way I started all my other days. I was accosted awake by my eager family members to get up and go to the bea...outlets? What? I thought to myself, we needed to go to the beach! And we needed to go now! We could shop later; this was my last day with Victor. It can't be cut short for some overcrowded mediocre shopping outlets. Why didn't they understand how important this day was to me? I immediately came up with a plan to make this go as fast as possible. We couldn't possibly take that long if I wasn't shopping, right? Wrong.

We got to the outlets, and the whole time, I was rushing them to go and get it done. My dad of course, being the pain in the ass that he was sometimes, decided to go into every store imaginable all because I was complaining to have them hurry up. He thought he was being funny when really he was wasting my precious time that I could be spending with Victor. My dad didn't care though, he took his sweet time, thus making us arrive at the beach a whopping five hours late seeing as we usually got to the beach around nine and we got there at two. I wanted to kill someone, I was so mad. Instead I just ripped off my cover up, failed to put on sunscreen, and bolted into the water. There was no time to waste. He greeted me as soon as I could reach him; I noted that he looked especially excited to see me. Maybe he was feeling the same way I was?

"What took you so long?" He asked jokingly but still kind of seriously. There was definitely a hidden urgency.

"My stupid parents just had to go shopping this morning." I replied with just a hint of anger in my tone.

"That sucks. By the way I have to leave at three," he told me with sadness in his tone.

"Crap, that means we only have a little less than an hour to hang out, what do you have to leave for?" I asked even angrier at my parents than I was before for taking so freaking long at the outlets.

"It's the last day with my grandparents so they are taking me and CeCe out to dinner with the rest of our family too," he explained. "But don't worry I'll come back to say goodbye one last time."

So we began the usual routine of talking about everything under the sun and when I would "forget" to tell him about a wave he'd go under water and flip me over. After what seemed like a quick conversation we got out of the water and joined Morgan and Zack to take pictures on the beach. We got one together and I promised to send a copy to him as soon as they got developed. We also exchanged e-mails and phone numbers so we could talk when we got back home. With that, we headed back out into the water. It's funny how you can get so used to a routine so quickly.

And it's so devastating when that routine is ripped away from you so quickly you don't even know what hit you. Sooner than we knew, CeCe came into the water to retrieve Victor and take him back to his grandparents. He murmured a quick goodbye and promised he would be back to give me a proper goodbye.

Approximately a half hour later, I turned around to face the beach, and low and behold, Victor was standing right there. I was so glad that he came back; I couldn't stand the thought of being away from him. I couldn't accept the fact that we lived over a thousand miles apart in the real world. In reality, I soon realized we didn't have a shot in hell of actually working out. We were too young and there were too many obstacles that would keep us from ever really being together.

"Hey babe, I want you to be the first and the last person that I say goodbye to, so get over here and hug me." He said with a certain confidence that I only wish I had.

I willingly obliged. Then I watched with much despair as he went around to the whole herd and said goodbye. He made his way back over to me and began what I will always describe as the most perfect moment in my life.

"Come here, you," he said gently.

He wrapped his arms around me; he was so much taller than me that they probably could have wrapped around twice. (I was skinny back then.) He pulled me in close and just held me there for a while. Then when we pulled apart a little bit he said, "You know I came up here for a family reunion and I didn't really have any reason to come back, until I met you."

Blushing, I smiled at him, choosing not to say anything because I didn't want to ruin this moment, I didn't want to ruin this feeling. He bent down and kissed my forehead, and then looked me in the eye and kissed me. His lips were soft and they fit nicely onto mine. With that kiss, I knew that I was done. I didn't want anyone else in the entire world. If all I had were that kiss, then that would be completely fine. I knew at that moment that I was in love with him more than I thought I was before. This time it was different though, because from that kiss alone, I knew he felt the exact same way I did. We were in love, it only took four days, I'd even argue less than that. It was amazing. He was amazing. I wanted this feeling for the rest of my life. I wanted him for the rest of my life.

He murmured a quick goodbye, and with that, he has gone. I watched him leave; every step away from me was a step towards reality. When he got to the pier, he turned and waved, and then, nothing. I was all alone again. The weight of the whole week hit me like a ton of bricks. I looked over at Zack and Morgan flirting in the water. Here I was boyless and getting a reality check that I just couldn't cash. When I looked over at Zack and Morgan, I could tell they were up to something. Then they started coming towards me.

"Hey Mary, want to do us a favor?" Morgan asked, her voice so sweet it made me want to vomit.

"Sure, what do you guys need?" I asked.

"Well we wanted to go for a walk but we know our parents would never let us go by ourselves so we were wondering if you would go with us?" Morgan asked in her sweetest of all tones. Of course I obliged. After all I had nothing better to do since Victor was gone for the day and probably forever. Now it was the tricky part, getting the parents on board with this little excursion idea.

"Hey momma, can Mary, Zack, and I go for a walk on the beach, please?" Morgan asked in her sweetest tone once again, she made sure to put my name first that way it didn't seem so suspicious.

"Yeah sure, as long as Mary is there to chaperone!" Aunt Laurie replied, apparently she wasn't as dumb as Morgan had thought but she still obliged, knowing that I wouldn't let anything too bad happen.

So off we went. I stayed near them until we were out of sight of the parents. Then I stayed closer to the shore looking for seashells to place in my locket. I wanted to get four. I knew this was an ambitious choice seeing as my locket was rather small but I knew what I wanted and I was determined to get it. What else was new? I was and still am such a type "A" personality. I kept looking and finally I stumbled upon them. They were small, just right even, as if they were meant for the locket. I took them near the water, completely draining out whatever Morgan and Zack were doing. I washed them off in the water, and then placed them in my locket, and yes all four fit. One for each of us to represent the most perfect vacation I was willing to bet that any of us had ever had.

As I sit here writing this, I occasionally look down and see that very locket, dangling from my neck. I know it seems silly but I can't help but wear it in remembrance of all that has happened between the four of us. It's more than a locket; it embodies a place where we actually stumbled upon true love, and I mean it when I say it, all of us fell in love. For some that love would mean forever, but as you'll find out, some would just be in love for now. It's hard to say looking back on it, even thinking about it ever ending, I still shiver when I think about it. But I suppose anything is possible and people can fall in love just as quickly as they can fall out of it. That's a sad matter though so lets stick to the good stuff.

Morgan and Zack were flirting obviously by the dunes; I could tell they had yet to kiss, so I decided to take matters into my own hands.

"Oh just do it already!" I screamed, the people around me had looks of confusion on their faces but I didn't care, I wanted Morgan to have the perfect moment too. I just didn't have the patience to let her acquire it on her own. It worked though, I saw them kiss but I quickly turned away so they could pretend like they were in a private place. For them I knew it would be a private place, a sacred place even, a place of new beginnings. Just like where Victor and I shared our moment, it was something that no one else could ever understand.

They came down near the shore were I was, and I was ready to engage them in conversation but they were both so quiet. Did I miss a fight or something? I figured they were just in awe of each other. Which was fine with me; I was so lost in thought about Victor that the rest of the world didn't really matter. As we were walking I saw Morgan grab Zack's arm, flip him towards her, and before you knew it, they were full on making out! Gross and a half!

That night, all of my thoughts drifted to Victor and the certain reality that we would have to face tomorrow. Oh and how I didn't want tomorrow to come! I wanted to live in that moment in the water. But progress needed to come and so it did. Little did I know that this might be the end of everything that I longed to be a part of.

Via Morgan
Chapter Ten: Go Pittsburgh!

I woke up really early that last morning. I knew that this was the end, and I wanted to spend every second possible with Zack. I woke up before most of my family in the house and got right into my bathing suit. I was ready to leave, right then and there. My mom and grandma were the only other ones up in my whole house. They were going shopping and for a tour of the island. They asked me to go with them. I wasn't sure. I took a long time to decide. Then I realized if I went with them, I wouldn't be sitting around waiting to leave. I knew it would take my mind off of Zack for a little bit. I thought it might have even cured some of my nerves and anticipation.

We were gone for a few hours. We drove through every street on the whole island, but all I could think of was 16th street. I wanted to get there; I needed to get there. I was stressed and nervous. When I finally got to the beach with my prettiest bathing suit on, it was about 10:30 a.m., I went straight for our spot in the water. He wasn't there. He didn't want to spend every second with me? I was hurt. I needed to be with him. Did he not realize that this was the last day?

After about an hour, I saw his mom. I swam over and asked her where Zack was. She told me he was fishing with his cousins and that he should be back soon. She was right. He got there about a half hour later. When he got there, it was just he, Victor, and I. We were just talking when Victor turned to Zack.

"So, Zack..."

"You chose now to do it?!" I said, freaking out. I swam away as quickly as possible. So I was sitting there about 100 feet away. I was bobbing my head up and down trying not to hear what's going on. I was so embarrassed. I was just trying to make it stop. I needed this moment to be over as quickly as possible. I was trying to calm myself down. After a few minutes of agony, I hear it. Zack and Victor were laughing. They're laughing at me!

"Wow I can hear you guys laughing at me from way out here!" I yelled to them. That was totally uncool.

Zack quickly swam over to me. He looked me in the eyes and said, "Don't worry, it's a good thing."

Such simple words. From those eyes, anything could have made me melt. He hit the spot, the spot deep in my heart. My complete humiliation didn't matter anymore. This was going to be a good day. I was sure of it.

A few hours later we were all together. We hadn't gotten out all day. It was then that I saw them. Clouds, big storm clouds were billowing in. It was going to be a big storm. Soon after, a huge boom shook the water, thunder. This was the end of a perfect day.

"Guys, that was thunder we should probably get out of the water!" I announced,

"No! That wasn't thunder! We don't have to get out of the water." Zack said. Rain fell, but we still didn't move.

Thinking back on it, I think Zack just didn't want to leave. If we got out of the water, we wouldn't be together. I like to think that's what he was thinking. Soon enough we were all out of the water. It was boot camp time. Uncle Joe insisted on boot camp, agility training, everyday. I made all of the Pittsburgh kids do it with us the last day. It was a "bonding moment," if you will. Lets just leave it at that. I'm not a runner and I never will be. I knew I was about to be completely humiliated in front of the guy I had fallen so deeply for in just four days.

After boot camp, we quickly jumped in the water to simple rinse off the sand from our bodies. Uncle Joe had made most of us fall while chasing us with a lacrosse stick in one and a beer in the other topped off with the safari hat on top. To put it nicely, it was a strange combination. When we were finally clean, we decided to take pictures. Mary and I ran around the beach making sure that we took as many pictures as possible. We knew that if we didn't the memories surely could fade. We took pictures together and with them.

Pittsburgh was then called away from their family. Their family vacation had become a vacation with Baltimore. They had one tradition that they wanted to keep in tacked. Every year they take a picture with all the kids on the beach on the last day. This year was different, though. Zack's mom wanted to get a picture with us Baltimore kids too.

We stood there as they took the picture. Mary and I stood a part from the group excluded. I actually think that we drew a circle around us so that no one would bother us in our very important boy talk. While in our own little circle, we wrote our names in the sand, and sealed it with a heart. It did not stay in plain sight for long. We covered it up quickly in hope that no one would look at us and think we were just stupid little girls. We covered it quickly leaving it engraved underneath the top layer. The four of our names were now apart of this island. It would always be deep down in the island, but more importantly it would be deep down within each of us.

After the torture, all of the kids returned to their post in the water. All of the kids were alone. This is when things heated up. Zack and I started talking serious. We started talking about people back home and our histories. I come to find out he had never kissed a girl. I was kind of surprised. I didn't understand how this great guy could slip through the cracks of so many girls. He was so perfect to me right then. Why didn't everyone else think he was perfect?

I think the reason he appealed to me was because of that. He was the opposite of Jeff. He was passive and laid back. Most importantly, he was innocent. He was exactly what I needed. He stabilized me. He taught me what I deserved. He taught me who I should be. He showed me how I should be treated and what I should feel. Jeff was the guy that tore me down. He was aggressive and as far from innocent as you could get. He didn't care about what I had to say. He knew what to say to get me to think just like he did. Zack, on the other hand, didn't want me to think like him. We were different, but we complimented each other. To this day, I am convinced that he saved me. He saved me from myself. I was a person who thought you could only get feelings for someone through physical actions. I was shocked that I could feel like this without doing anything. I wanted to show him something too. I wanted to make sure he remembered me somehow. I wanted him, I wanted to seal that he was mine.

We talked about it and we both wanted it. (By "it" I mean we wanted to kiss.) We needed it to happen. The only thing was how, and where? Both of our families were around. That is not romantic! We decided a walk would be the best way to get away; we took Mary with us to make it not so obvious, I think everyone knew anyway. As we were walking, we got into one of our little dumb fights. It was over the word "on." We say it two different ways, the Pittsburgh way and the right way aka the Baltimore way. Now, the Pittsburgh way is something like "Ah-n", whereas in Baltimore it is said something like "Ow-n." We were both really stubborn and needless to say we were yelling at each other. Finally after a good five minutes, I say:

"Fine, why don't you go ask a random person on the beach!"

So he did, "Excuse me, I know this is really random, and I'm sorry to interrupt you, but how do you say the word 'O-N'?"

They agreed with him. He begins to explain our whole life story. "Thank you, I was right! Sorry, I'm from Pittsburgh and she's from Baltimore and we couldn't come to an agreement of who was right and just proved me right, so thank you!"

"Oh really? Pittsburgh? What part? We're from Pittsburgh too!" The sweet couple announced.

"No way! You cheated. Not fair!" I was furious. I couldn't believe that it was coincidence that the people he picked were from Pittsburgh. It was though. What are the odds!

We walked away after a good ten minutes of talking to those people. We walked along the beach nervously. What would happen? Would it seal the feelings? What if it's not good and there is nothing there? We walked silently, both in deep thought.

Finally, we got there. We got to where no one was. Where the houses ended and it was vacant of all human life except for us. Mary, who had been at the shoreline the whole time, made a comment about getting it over with. It was now or never, and we chose now. We walked toward the dunes and stopped on a little hill. We came in really close, and closed our eyes. It was then his lips that first touched mine. Our lips were butchered from hours in the water and exposure to the sun. The kiss was dry and short. There were no fireworks. It felt dead and forced. It was a complete letdown. The one thing that I thought would make me so happy had actually left me feeling completely terrible.

I didn't want that to be the way I remembered him. I needed to feel those fireworks. I couldn't say goodbye to him until I did. But when could I do this? We had already started walking back. By the time we got halfway back I couldn't take it anymore. I had to do something about it. I had to take matters into my own hands. I turned to him. I grabbed his arm and pull him into me.

"What?" he said with an attitude.

Right after he said that, he realized what I was doing. Right there in the middle of the beach we had the most passionate kiss. (Okay I'm over exaggerating, but it was still kind of passionate.) I felt it. The fireworks were there. It was perfect. We would probably still be there in that kiss if it weren't for an interruption.

"Go Pittsburgh!" A loud cheer came from about twenty feet away.

It was the people we had met when he asked about "on." We had been right in front of them. We didn't know what to do but laugh.

Hand in hand, we walked. The two most important people in my life and I walking knowing that life just couldn't get any better than it was right then. The world for a minute stood still, until we finally got back to reality.

Our reality was getting back to our herd. However, everything was different now. We were different. It was like we had stepped into an alternate universe where everything was flipped upside down. We were in love. We desperately hoped that the parents wouldn't notice. Well, he actually was the one hoping. He knew his parents wouldn't be okay with it. He knew I had to be a secret, but I wanted to tell the world.

Luckily we didn't have to see a soul. There was no one on the beach. All the kids were exactly where we had left them, in the same circle in the middle of the ocean. The weird thing was the adults were missing. The only moving they ever made from their semi-circle of beach chairs was to get up and walk to the cooler for another beer. Something was weird. That is when the three of us looked out into the ocean and saw that large orange and blue oasis floating in the ocean. The kids weren't on it. Then I remembered what my mother had said days before, "That thing is great we could shove the elders on there with food and ship them off to sea so we don't have to deal with them. It's like an adult playpen." (Oh and that's where the name came from.) That's where they had to be. We could be alone for a little bit longer.

However, the alone time was short lived. The adults come out of the water panting. They couldn't handle the wild ride of the adult playpen. I guess the adult playpen really wasn't meant for adults.

67

"We better get home. The sun is going down. Its about 8." says my mom with a heavy exhale after every word. The words broke my heart. Somehow the day had slipped away from us, and so had the week. This was the time to say goodbye. The week and the romance were over.

I walked down the line and hugged his whole family. They had become kind of like my family. We talked about keeping in touch and potential trips up to that awful city to visit each other. I went to everyone but him. I thought maybe I could prolong the process of saying goodbye so maybe it wouldn't hurt as bad as I thought it would. But the clock had ticked one too many times and it was now or never. Screw it, I thought. It'll be easier to just leave it like this and not say goodbye. Then I realized I would regret it forever.

I found him knee-deep in the ocean. I knew people were watching so I realized nothing was going to happen. We just simply said goodbye, nothing else. We hugged and then it was over. All I needed was one more kiss, but I knew I couldn't have that. I turned away knowing I would not see him for 358 more days.

As I walked up the pier, I turned and took one last look at the beach that had changed my life. I saw everything. The first thing that I saw was the red and white striped umbrella that had started this whole thing. The only red and white umbrella on the beach. Every time I saw it I knew that this was real. I knew that he would always be sitting there under that umbrella waiting for me. I relived all the things that happened that day and the four previous days and I felt a wet teardrop fall down my cheek. From that moment until I had walked 100 yards to the Rosario's beach house, I realized my whole world.

I realized that everything was over. In a month we were both starting a new school. We were starting in high school. We were going to change. Our lives would be changing, and by the time we would have returned back to this very spot we would not know each other. Our brand new lives would ruin us. We wouldn't know each other in 52 weeks. So from the one hundred yard walk, I realized my life was over, well our life together was over.

I got to the Rosario's and washed my feet off. I couldn't stand any longer; my legs were weakened by the realization that he would never be in my life again. I got my bag, sat at the steps away from everyone, and plugged in my iPod. I needed to drain out everyone's voice except the voice inside my own head.

I sat there for about twenty minutes waiting for all the chairs to be washed and packed up in to the car, but my parents had made no progress. That is when I heard it, though. I heard him and his cousins next door just messing around and laughing. How can he be laughing and having a good time when I was sitting here so upset, I thought to myself. I decided to go over there and let him know what I was thinking and what I was feeling. I walked across the bushes and called him over.

He walked right up to me with a big smile on his face, and put his arm right around me. I can still hear him say, "What's up babe?"

I went off on a tangent with tears in my eyes, "I'm just really upset. I'm not going to see you ever again. And just everything is never going to be the same. I'll never talk to you again. All I want to do is talk to you. We had such a great week, I just don't want to lose you."

"Babe, chill I'm going to see you in a year." With that one sentence, he made the tears stop. Now I realize he obviously thought I was just a crazy little girl being super clingy, but in the moment it was the perfect thing for him to say to me. He was just comforting me. It was like he was so confident that nothing was going to change us and in a year everything would be even better than it was now. From that moment on I chose to forget what I had realized. I chose to forget that I knew how it would end and to believe this great person who had changed me in just a few short days.

I walked back through the bushes back into the world of sadness. I saw Mary sitting on the rock driveway with her iPod in, all alone. I went up to her and just sat down. Neither of us spoke to each other. We just sat there in our thoughts, just wondering what the future will hold for our guys and us.

Via Mary
Chapter Eleven: You've Got Mail

Two days, it had been two days since I last spoke to him. Since I last saw him. Since he last held me in his arms. Oh how I missed those arms. Those eyes. That face. Everything about him. After I got home from the beach, I showed up on Morgan's doorstep. I couldn't be alone. Not now, not when my heart lay in such a potentially destructive situation. So for two days straight we laid in her computer room compulsively checking our e-mails and AIM systems waiting to hear from them. We needed so badly to have them reach out to us. We needed to know that they were just as in love with us and we were with them. And trust me, this was love, I was more sure of that than anything else in my entire life. Sometimes Morgan and I would go out and lay in her hammock to get out of the house for a little bit. But we continued to obsess over our vacation. The vacation that had shaped us into completely different people than we were going into it. We so longed to be with them. We knew for certain that we were irrevocably in love with them. We knew we would know them all of our lives.

Then it happened, Morgan's phone vibrated, a sign of hope. It was Zack, he had actually texted her. It was brief but it was enough to fill her heart with hope. As for me? Nothing. There was no sign of Victor at all. All I wanted was a silly little e-mail or a phone call, anything, just a sign of life to know that I wasn't half as crazy as I was feeling. I checked my e-mail again, nothing. Where was he?! I didn't understand. I thought that we really meant something to each other. I though this was really love. Was I wrong? Was it really too good to be true? Why didn't he crave me in his life?

Another day passed, this meant it was day three. I woke up around eleven in the morning. What can I say? I am a late sleeper! I ran downstairs to check my e-mail; all I was hoping for was a message, anything to know that he still wanted to be with me! I typed my password with much enthusiasm. This was going to be the day that I heard from him! I just knew it in my heart. There it was, a new e-mail. I didn't recognize the name but I opened it with hope. I looked immediately at the name. It was him! He really wrote me:

> *Subject: You*
> *Sent: Wed 8/10/05*
> *I miss you a bunch. The beach was amazing I remember everything about it. I didn't like how you went shopping for so long that one day. We could have spent more time together. O well.*
>
> *Much love from your man,*
> *Victor*

I wrote him back with all the enthusiasm I had ever had in my life I wanted him to know that I was in this for all of time. I wanted him to know that I loved him, that I cared, and that I would be waiting for him until I saw him again. This e-mail was like life or death to me, every word, every comma, period, and exclamation point mattered. Now that I knew him, I wondered how I had ever made it through life without him. He was becoming such a big part of who I was. I was finally letting my guard down and letting myself get lost in him. And for the first time in my life, that was okay. I was okay with him being such a big part of who I was. To be honest, now that I knew him, I wouldn't have it any other way. He may not have been all of me but damn he was growing on me. I was elated because later that day he wrote again.

> *Subject: I Love You*
> *Sent: Wed 8/10/05*
> *I understand that your dad had plans. I still got to see you so it was cool. Thanks for going fast. I hope everything is good in Maryland. Give me some details.*
>
> *Love, Victor*

It wasn't much but it was enough for me. He was all I needed, and now I knew, due to the subject headline that he was just as much in love with me as I was with him. This was real, I told myself. It wasn't just a dream that vacation actually happened. I was so glad for it too. I couldn't imagine life without him. And from that day on, my inbox was peppered with more emails from the boy, who would soon become the man I would love all of my life. A few of my favorites were:

> *Subject: I love you so much. You are all I think about*
> *Sent: Wed 8/17/05 6:05 PM*
> *All I have been thinking about is you. You are so amazing. I'll keep looking at your pics on you myspace. I sound obsessed about you. I can't wait to see you.*
>
> *Love your man,*
> *Victor*

> *Subject: I LOVE YOU*
> *Sent: Mon 8/29/05 8:00 PM*
> *I love you sooo much you are the only person I think about. I'm glad Katrina missed us. I'm watching everything on the news about it. Keep writing.*
>
> *Love your man,*
> *Victor*

> *Subject: Hey*
> *Sent: Wed 12/07/05 6:26 PM*
> *I'm sorry I haven't talked to you in a long time. I had a dream about you all last night, I know kinda random but oh well. I can't wait to see you again. I need to call you some time. I love you, and I can't wait until the next time I will see you.*
>
> *Love,*
> *Victor*
> *P.S.—You look hot in your pictures*

Those are just a few of my favorite emails from him and yes I am probably embarrassing him by putting them into the book but he loves me enough to let him slide. As I look back on these e-mails, I still to this day (Sept 2, 2009) get a huge dumb grin on my face as I can't help but smile when I look back on emails from the man that I have loved all along.

Via Morgan
Chapter Twelve: The Final Step

Finally everything was packed and it was time to leave. It was time for us to leave the beach for Summerville one last time. Half of my family was already in the house and showered. I got home and dinner was on the table, so we ate it. After dinner I went down stairs to the outdoor shower to take my last shower. I couldn't seem to take all of these lasts. It wasn't fair. It had all came just too soon. I just wanted some more time. All the emotions came back to me when I heard a noise outside the shower. I couldn't help but hope it was Zack coming back to talk to me again. I realized it couldn't be him, and after that I couldn't determine the shower waters from my tears. He was gone.

After my shower, my mom tried to motivate me to pack because she needed to pack up the car. I left my phone on the kitchen table to prevent myself from getting upset from it not ringing and hearing him on the other end of it. I headed up the green hardwood stairs to my room to empty out those white dresser drawers into my blue and white paisley Vera Bradley duffle bag. I just couldn't do it though. After every article I put in the bag, I had to stop for a few minutes to cry.

I couldn't hear anything except my tears for about an hour. At times I would hear yelling of my cousin Nick and my sister. (They fight a lot) But mostly it was just tears. In between one of my heaving I heard it. The distant singing of "It's 5 O'clock Somewhere." That was my ring tone at that point.

I've never been a runner. But that night I was! My tears stopped immediately, and I got straight up and was out of that room within fifteen seconds. I have never run down a flight of steps so fast in my life. I ran right to my phone and looked at it, and saw my dreams coming true. It read three missed calls from Zack. I don't think I've ever been that happy in my life. I called my voicemail and I heard his voice. "Hey. I'm going ghost crab fishing. Want to come up and come with me?"

Thank you God! He wanted to see me again. I didn't care what I had to do to get there I was seeing him one more time. It meant everything to me that he wanted to see me again! I ran up to my parents. "Can you take me to Zack's, or Ashley?"

They killed it. They had killed every sense of hope in my body. I felt like falling to the ground and crying for a lifetime. "Morgan, really? We are leaving tomorrow and we must pack the car."

That shot an idea into my head. I couldn't drive but I could walk. The bikes had already been brought back to Julie's Bike Shop, so it was just walking. "Well, can I walk them?" I said in desperate hope for that three-letter word I was yearning for, yes.

I didn't get what I was looking for though. "It is 9 o'clock at night you cannot walk that far by yourself. It's dark out. Are you crazy?"

"Why not? Jesus! I'm freaking 14! I'm not a little kid anymore. It's not that big of a deal. I can walk 30 blocks! Please, I really need to see him." They rolled their eyes. That's what they do when they're annoyed and you should just give up because it isn't working. "Fine. You're ruining my life. I might die if you don't let me go. Like, I literally like might like kill myself if you don't like let me go." I said like a lot at the age of 14. I thought it made me sound cool, but I was very wrong. Anyways, they rolled their eyes one more time. I needed another plan of attack. That is when it hit me. "Well, if I can't go alone then that means you'll let me go with someone. Can Ashley come with me?"

My mom half rolled her eyes. "Fine, if you can get your sister to go, you can go if you finish packing and stop bothering me." YES. I had won. It was the first time in my life that I, the middle child, had gotten what I wanted. It was definitely a personal victory.

The only problem was that Ashley was stuck to her phone being a self-centered 16-year-old girl talking to the boy of the week, Antonio. That's when it hit me; my mom was setting me up. She knew for a fact that Ashley would never in a million years go for it. I begged and begged for her to come with me. She didn't accept until I offered her $30. She could not resist that.

I ran up the stairs one last time into the second room on the right. That was Aunt Robin's room where my clothes were being held. I threw as many clothes into my Vera as possible. They were all in a huge ball which made it pretty difficult to close it. I didn't care, though, because I was going to see Zack one more time.

As soon as I was done, I heard the phone ring again. I felt my spirits lift even further and felt that grin coming back. I looked at the phone, but didn't see Zack's name. The name that came up on that trashy old phone read "Jeff." I reluctantly picked up the phone and said hello. "Hey baby. What are you doing? Why havn't I talked to you in a few days? You said you were going to call."

"Sorry. I've been hanging out with that guy a lot. I'm actually going to go hang out with him right now." I snapped back at him.

"Oh really? Why? When I went on vacation, I didn't meet anyone new. So why the hell do you think that you can? You are so inconsiderate to my feelings. Whatever, you are just going to come crawling back to me as soon as you get home. He is just not as good as me and you will realize that tomorrow." He said with an attitude.

"Well actually he is better than you. He is kind and sweet. He is like no one I have ever met before. He is perfect. You will never be as good as him. We had a perfect day together. I was his first kiss, and it was perfect. So I wouldn't be so confident about that."

"He's never kissed someone before! Are you serious? Now I know I have nothing to worry about. Girl, you have needs and I satisfy them, and obviously, he can't. You will come back to me.

"Jeff, I do not care what you think. You should have something to worry about. Goodbye." I said bitterly as I slammed the phone down onto the phone. How dare he say those things. He knew nothing about Zack, and he never would. I felt a strange sense of relief. I felt like it was over for good this time. I had finally gotten rid of him. There was now nothing that could hold me back with Zack. I realized that it took me until now, when I was packing to leave him, that I felt comfortable enough to give him everything I had. I waited until it was basically over. All I had was one more walk which was about to take place. I wished that I could sit there and wait so that I couldn't have to leave him forever. I knew that if I did wait I may never get to have that time with him.

It was time to be on our way. My legs were shaking in excitement, and I thought I wouldn't be able to make it. Before I left, I think I looked in the mirror about 15 minutes making sure I looked okay. Oh my god, this is the first time he will every see me with clothes on. What if he doesn't like me not almost naked? Only now does it dawn on me how backwards that thought was.

My sister and I have had a weird relationship my whole life. We hated each other until I was twelve, and when I say hated, I mean it. She used to pinch me and I used to throw her down flights of stairs. (But that is still a touchy situation even fifteen years later.) From the age of twelve all the way to the present, we have I guess you would call it a love/hate kind of relationship. We can talk about anything, and she will protect me and back me up no matter what. However, we can fight like the worst of enemies. We had fought right before we left because she didn't wanted to go but once she realized how much it meant to me she was on board. We ended up talking and laughing the whole walk. We talked about high school, the beach, and most importantly, boys. I could tell her anything and she could too. She would tell me her horror stories to make sure I didn't make the same mistakes she did.

We got about half way. We were on about 6th street. We saw a parked car with headlights and those stupid blue lights underneath. When we got closer we realized there were two people in the car, probably in their early twenties, and then there was one outside of the car. We thought it was rather sketchy, so we tried to walk quickly so we didn't have to have an altercation with them. Unfortunately, that failed. All of a sudden we heard an exploding bass coming from the car. It was a beat we were oh too familiar with. The words came on, "Hey how you doin lil mama? lemme whisper in your ear Tell you sumthing that you might like to hear You got a sexy ass body and your ass look soft Mind if I touch it? And see if its soft Naw I'm jus playin' unless you say I can And I'm known to be a real nasty man And they say a closed mouth don't get fed So I don't mind asking for head You heard what I said, we need to make our way to the bed And you can start usin' yo head You like to fuck, have your legs open all in da butt Do it up slappin ass cause the sex gets rough Switch the positions and ready to get down to business So you can see what you've been missin'" The Ying Yang's new hit was blaring through the speakers. We knew that it wasn't going to be good now. Something was going to happen I could feel it

"Hey ladies," said the extremely intoxicated girl in the front seat. "You guys are hot! Come on over and party with us. You're really hot! I'm a lesbian! Come on its okay because I'm a lesbian. Are you guys because you're really hot I want to party with you two?" We walked quickly away afraid that she would follow us.

After that I wasn't nervous at all. The crazy drunk lesbian had taken my away all of nerves and I knew know that I was going to be okay to see him. I could do this now. I survived a lesbian; I can survive seeing the love of my life again.

Before I knew it I was standing right in front of his house. It was now or never. I called his phone and waited a good eight minutes for him to actually come to the phone after his mom answered the phone. Finally the wait was over, "Hey, what's up?"

"I'm here. Where are you?"

"Oh why didn't you just come up? I'll come down and meet you down underneath the house." I stood and waited for him to come down. Finally, through the darkness, I saw a white shirt emerge. Once he got closer I realized what he was wearing. He was wearing a number seven Pittsburgh Steelers jersey, Ben Roethlisberger.

"Did you really wear that? I'm going home right now." I said jokingly before I even said hello. The Steelers was his only flaw at that point and he was bragging about it. I was ready to leave at that point.

"Oh shut up. You so love it. You are just jealous you don't have a jersey as awesome as this one. You know you want to stay. You do not want to leave," he said oh too confidently.

We walked up the back steps onto the porch. Scotty and Megan were sitting there playing poker and flirting more than I have ever seen two people flirt. (That was the start of their two-year romance.) He pulled up two chairs in the corner and we just sat there. We just sat there, but for that I was glad. Ashley and I had taken too long to walk, so we had missed the ghost-crab fishing. I had wanted to spend time just with him anyway. Ashley stayed down the steps on the phone with her lasted catch. She really had no interest in being there. She didn't care what I was doing. She knew I was in good hands. Zack was the first and only guy I have ever been interested in that she actually liked.

All of a sudden I felt heaviness on my hand. I looked down and saw his hand on top of mine. I felt my breath slip away from me. I was so surprised and so happy it was like everything was finally coming together. All of my stresses and heartaches just left and in that moment, everything was okay in the world.

I sat in that wooden chair for at least ten minutes just trying to touch the ground of after flying. In ten minutes I had not spoken, took a real breath, or even blink. It felt like every muscle in my body had frozen. They were in shock and were not sure if it was this was an okay thing. The muscles in my hand were screaming to my brain, "We've never felt anything like this. Is this normal, or should I run?"

"Get out!" yelled my head.

But finally the voice of reason chimed into the debate. For the first time I listened to what I wanted, and I realized what I deserved. Affection was what I needed and deserved. Abuse didn't have to be there. It was possible to have an authentic loving relationship.

The words spoken that night will never be remembered. They were not worth remembering. They were nothing special, but I did not mind. I needed just buffer time with him before it was really over for good.

Before I knew it, Ashley was coming up the porch stairs. "Morg, we have to be back in a half and hour we better go. You know how long it will take us to get back." And with that it was time to go through saying goodbye to him one more time.

He walked me down the stairs, and gently kissed me goodbye. With that it was done. There was no more possible hope for us seeing each other any longer. I met Ashley at the end of the rocky driveway, and began walking down the empty street. In a small quite island like this its dead on the streets by ten and by now it was at least 11:30. There was nothing to talk about and there was nothing to see on the streets. I just looked at the moon just thinking that he was looking at the moon too, and somehow he was gone anymore.

I was just thinking about the night, and seeing him appear in the darkness when I remembered that we had brought a flashlight with us. "Just leave it there its not that big of a deal it's a flashlight, Morgan. We will call the Rosario's when we get back and we will go over there when we get home." proclaimed my lazy sister who just didn't want to walk back.

"No Ashley, I have to get it now." I just wanted an excuse to go back and see him just one more time. I would not have been able to live with myself if I had had the opportunity and I did not capitalize on that. "I'll just run and go get it real quick."

I was only a block or two away so I jogged on back with the biggest smile on my face. When I reached the house all I heard was "She's back." Zack's twin cousin Bubby and Kate, yelled. They were twelve then and pulled him down the steps towards me, and then stayed on the steps to watch what we were doing.

"I just forgot my flashlight." He went back up the stairs and grabbed it for me and handed it right to me. Somehow I got tangled up in his eyes and ended up stuck to his lips. For the first time I felt passion behind a kiss. I had had millions of kisses but nothing that meant anything like that. That was the real thing. Goodbye was the only other thing that was said, after the third time one word seems to do the trick. I walked away, never to look back.

I caught up to my sister and regained my post of staring at the moon. I was lost in my thoughts and the next thing I knew, I was at the doorsteps of Summerville. I did not say a word to anyone, just simply walked up to my bed, turned on my iPod, and went to sleep.

Via Mary
Chapter Thirteen: Holding Strong

Our first year together was blissful. We talked on the phone almost every day for about two to four hours. I know what could we possibly have to talk about for that long every day? It was unheard of, and the ever-rising phone bill was annoying our parents. My parents finally saw the light and got a long-distance plan that enabled us to talk whenever we wanted so long as I called him. Which was fine by me so long as I could talk to him. And talk we did. About everything under the sun, we talked about our favorite things, what we didn't so much like, marriage, families, where we would live, all of it. It was wonderful to hear his voice every day. I never took it for granted either because with so much distance between us, this was the only way to keep us connected.

The other cool thing was we didn't just talk to each other. We talked to each other's parents, and I even began to develop a friendship with his younger sister, Cece. Cece, by the way, is to this day one of my most near and dear friends. She has helped me through Victor's new situation. I couldn't be more thankful to have her in my life and to be able to call her one of my greatest friends. Even if she tries to take videos of me singing the Jonas Brothers songs on video chat. In any event, I got to talk to some of his friends, too. They were great and some of them even felt comfortable enough to call me when they weren't even with Victor. His friends were actually becoming my friends too just as mine were becoming his.

We told each other everything too. The big thing was that I was in my sophomore year of high school and even though we were the same age he was in his freshman year of high school. Because of that we made our relationship open in that if we wanted to date someone else we could so long as we were honest about it. This system made sense only because he was just starting high school and I didn't want him to have to go alone to dances and other events just because he was dating me. That didn't seem fair and I didn't want him to begin to resent me for holding him back. This system seemed to work well.

Specific details about the first year are all starting to blur and fade away altogether, which is heart breaking. But I do believe that there was more love and care between the two of us in that one-year than most people would see in their entire lives together. I couldn't imagine being with anyone else, even though I was rarely even physically with him. That never mattered; to this day it still doesn't matter. I had always heard that absence makes the heart grow fonder but I never really understood that until I stumbled upon my relationship with Victor. Most thought us to be crazy, saying that it would never last. They didn't understand how five days could be so powerful and draw two complete strangers so close together. All the time I would have to endure comments about how I was stupid to drag this on. "Let it go," my friends from home would prod, insisting it was just an overdone summer fling. I guess I wasn't much help either because I couldn't explain to them why I was so drawn to him, all that I knew is that I was. So no matter how many times they begged me to come out and party and hang out with other boys, I just didn't. I'd much rather stay in and cuddle up on the phone with the one that I truly believed was made for me, just as I was made for him. Some of my more outgoing friends got frustrated with me. And I don't blame them, because to the common person, it doesn't make any sense.

The thing about love though is it doesn't need to make sense. Nothing needs to make sense. As long as you have that other person, that's all that matters. We were crazy about each other. We didn't need anyone else. Which is kind of ironic because as wrapped up in each other as we were we made sure to have separate lives as well. As if a long distance relationship wasn't unhealthy enough, one without a support system would be so much worse. So we made sure that we were spending ample time with our friends because if we did break up, as unspeakable as that may have sounded we needed to have some sort of semblance of a life to come back to.

So we would continue on our journey, our lives merged together so perfectly. It seemed as though nothing could come between us. We loved each other more than anything else in the whole world, what could go wrong?

Via Morgan
Chapter Fourteen: Dead Hearts

I woke up just a few hours later to the sound of cleaning and packing. It was time to leave. I went into the bathroom, and looked at myself for the first time with new eyes. Life from now on was going to be different. I splashed water on my face in hopes of getting all the tears out before I got into a car for eight hours with my family, and then I brushed my teeth. I walked downstairs and tried to think of an excuse not to leave. I thought about nailing myself down the floor. Then maybe this could continue. Instead, I went down below the house and sat on the picnic table next to our car, and I just waiting to leave. I only shed one tear. I told myself that there was nothing to upset about. It was the best week of my life.

When we finally loaded ourselves into the car, I was asleep before we left the island. I couldn't stand to watch Sunset Beach slip away. I slept 7 hours and 45 minutes of the eight-hour trip. I woke up and I was back in good old Reisterstown, Maryland. Once we reached a road called 795, just a highway meant to get you from Pikesville to Reisterstown, which was all of 8 miles long, I could not tell myself it was okay any longer. I was home. I was back to reality. (For a whole week I couldn't manage to go on that road without crying.) It was on 795 where I picked up my phone and read a message from Zack. "So, we are in Morgantown and it made me think of you."

Finally, our Acura drove up that oh too familiar driveway. I saw my grandma mowing the lawn by my childhood swing set that read "Ashley, Morgan, and RJ's kingdom," and my golden retriever, Angeli, barking and jumping in excitement that we had returned. Everyone was glad to be home except me. It was real now. I was back to the place I had to pretend was my home for 51 weeks.

I ran up the stairs, completely neglecting my parents screaming my name to help unpack the car. I ran straight to my bed without turning back. I kicked off my shoes and rolled up against my pillow hoping that this would be my permanent position for the next 51 weeks.

I caught a glance at my newly shoeless feet, however. They were all cut up from all of the running on the beach that was so unnecessarily forced upon me. I just sat there picking off the dead skin. I had a huge piece of hanging skin on the ball of my right foot. I manipulated it and eventually ripped it off with no tools except my fingers. It started to bleed a little. That is when I saw it. The redness in the blood just made it pop even more. The crevice where the dead skin used to be had now formed a heart.

This was fate. The rain falling from two feet above soon diluted the blood. This must mean something. It was the ending to a perfect week. I couldn't help but feel like it was a special tattoo, a tattoo from God. God was telling me that there was nothing to regret, and that there was nothing to be scared of because everything would work out. It just had to. I mean, it was written on my foot! I hoped it would never fade away. I hoped it would be a permanent reminder of Zack and Sunset Beach as a whole.

I was in bliss, shock, and even a state of depression. How was I supposed to feel? I had never felt so strongly about someone, and surely had never had it taken away from me. How was I supposed to begin to go back to the life that I saw out of my bedroom window? The only life I knew how to live was a life with the

Kindred Spirit watching over me as the warm but refreshing waves crashed into my thighs.

I was home for maybe an hour when Mary showed up at my doorstep. "I don't want to be alone. Can we hang out? Maybe just lay around and talk?" How could I say no she looked like she just died and came back to life, plus that's exactly what I needed too? She didn't leave for two days.

For two days, we sat by our phones and by the computer waiting for Zack or Victor to try and contact us. We slept on the floor, and didn't say much. We knew what the other one was thinking and feeling, but we didn't know how to fix it or what to say because we knew there was nothing we could say to solve our mutual problem. Zack sent me one text but that was more than Mary could say. She received nothing from Victor and she was a mess.

All we could do was sit there and think of everything that we would be losing. Our tans would peel off, first. Next, their accents and voices would leave our minds. After a few more weeks, the picture in our minds of them would go and we would not be able to remember what the most important people in our lives looked like any more. The worst of it all, however, we knew that one day the memories of Zack and Victor would no longer exist. All we could do was feel everything slowly melt away until nothing was left except four broken hearts.

Via Mary
Chapter Fifteen: The Fight

Before I knew it, our world would be crashing down upon us. Life, as we knew it would cease to be as we remembered it. All it would take is one simple phone call and us would become he and I. There would be no more "we" and no more "us." How foolish we were and oh how are folly would destroy us. This would be the cause of a new chapter that neither of us ever even dreamed of opening. Life would change again, and when we got used to that change another would follow. So let me tell you a story of disaster that started with the ringing of my phone.

"Hello?" I answered, I probably shouldn't have picked it up in the first place because I didn't recognize the number but curiosity got the best of me and I answered anyway.

"Hey Mary, it's Jamie, Victor's friend," said the voice on the other line.

"Oh hey, how are you?" I answered; relieved to know whom I was talking to.

"I'm good, I'm good, just hanging out, what about you?" she asked ominously, like she was about to tell me something that would rock my world.

"I'm great, I actually just got off of the phone with Victor," I said probably overly cheery, though I didn't know that my mood would swiftly change.

"Yeah that's good to hear, so speaking of Victor, did he happen to tell you anything about us?" she asked with just a hint of deceit in her tone.

"Um no, why? What's going on?" I asked, beginning to get anxious, I didn't like were this was going in the least.

"Oh well it's nothing, never mind." She said coolly.

"Are you sure, I mean you can tell me anything, I really don't mind." I said, hoping she would tell me whatever it was that was on her mind.

"Well I mean it's no big deal, him and I just hooked up," she remarked as if it were nothing. But I wasn't going to let her know how much this hurt me. I was determined to play it cool when really I was freaking out on the inside.

"Oh okay, that's cool." I said, it killed me to act so calm but I did it anyway.

"Anyways, I have to go but I just thought you should know, I'll talk to you later. Bye!" Before I could say anything the line was silent.

For the next few minutes, all I could do was pace around my house attempting to calm down but all I really did was freak out even more. How could he do this to me? I mean, we always said that if we hooked up with other people, we would be honest and tell each other. Yet here we were already failing to do so, well at least he was. To be honest I was livid and I didn't know what to do. I wasn't sure if I should call him and scream at him or follow my first instinct, which was to call Morgan. So I did. Five rings and it went to voicemail, which I was too angry to leave one so I just hung up. She'd call back when she got the chance. I knew I should call him and straighten things out but I was raging with anger so I decided to wait until I cooled down, for his sake. It takes a lot to get me mad, but boy when someone does it, I get angry and it's a scary sight to see.

Twenty minutes later my phone rang and luckily I recognized the phone number and answered it within the first two rings.

"Hey girl, you called?" said a familiar voice, which belonged to none other than my best friend Morgan.

"Oh girl you called at the wrong time, I am livid," I said, my voice teeming with anger.

"Okay calm down, I'm coming over," she said. She was another one who wouldn't let me say goodbye because by the time I was going to protest, the line was again silent. What was it with girls these days? So impatient, I swear!

About ten minutes later, there was a knock on my door, and when I went to open it I was swallowed up in Morgan's arms. Something I needed more than I cared to admit. She didn't let go right away either, again something I needed more than either of us would admit.

"Okay so spill, what happened?" she asked, as she plopped down on the couch, I was still too angry to sit, so I paced around the living room floor as I recounted the phone call. By the end of it I was so angry I was practically screaming at Morgan even though she did nothing wrong.

"That bitch!" Morgan half yelled. Our moms were outside talking, so she made sure to not be too loud. I wasn't sure whom she was referring to at this point because I considered both of them to be little bitches. I was pissed, and Morgan now understanding my side of the story, was getting pretty angry herself.

"I know and its not like I can just call him out on it, what the hell am I supposed to do, just wait around for his sorry ass to fess up? You know he won't! God I just hate him sometimes!" I practically yelled.

"Seriously, who the fuck does he think he is? Some kind of Casanova! Screw that! Girl you should just call him and yell at him, that's what I'd do!" Morgan practically yelled right back.

"Nah I don't want to yell, that'll make me look like a jealous bitch, I'd rather just wait for him to come crawling to me, and trust me, he better do just that or there are going to be some major problems," I said, trying to hold it together.

"Do you think he'll actually tell you though?" Morgan asked, trying to be logical.

"You're right, how about I wait for him to call me, and when he does, I'll just talk to him about it. I'm sure he'll just tell me it was a mistake or something, there is no way he can actually like that, that skank" I said, beginning to cool off.

I continued to pace around the room, not quite ready to sit down and take a load off. Morgan and I continued to discuss strategy. We decided that I, unlike him, would handle this the mature way and wait for him to call, and when he did, I would bring it up if he didn't in a reasonable amount of time. We would be grown ups and discuss what happened and he would give me a good explanation as to why he didn't tell me sooner. This would be short and simple, right? Wrong. It never went this way, not when there were emotions getting involved. This was bound to be an all-out war, a battle of the sexes if you will. And I was determined to win. You see I don't like to yell. So naturally I don't do it very often. Therefore when I do yell it means something. Oh and he had it coming more than he could ever fathom.

Our conversation about rationality and reason got interrupted because yet again my phone rang. Speak of the devil it was Victor! I debated answering it, I wasn't sure if I was ready to get into it with him. But being the headstrong person that I was, I went ahead and answered it anyway.

"What?" I half screamed into the phone.

"Um, hi to you too?" he answered, not yet knowing the disaster that was about to take place.

"So, when were you going to tell me about Jamie" I asked so acidically I could have burned the receiver.

"What are you talking about?" he asked, there was a certain honesty in his tone that made me almost stop being mad, but I continued on.

"Well I got a little phone call from our friend Jamie today and she just so happened to mention that you two hooked up, want to explain that a little bit. Huh? Do you? Or were you planning on me never finding out?" I spat back at him.

"Mary." Was all he could manage to get out.

"What?" I said again, only this time it was a full on scream. I was more livid than I had ever been.

"I'm so sorry, I can't believe she told you this way, I was going to tell you, really, I was. I just hadn't gotten a chance." He was trying to remain calm though obviously thrown off by my anger.

"Whatever, I hate you I can't believe you would do this, it's two weeks before I was going to see you again and you couldn't even wait to see me you just had to hook up with her?" I screamed. Morgan grabbed my arm and tried to get me to calm down but there was no stopping me, not when I was like this. I'd never felt so betrayed in my life.

"Mary I'm sorry, I never meant to hurt you like this, what can I do to make it up to you, I mean I'm going to see you in a few weeks, can't you just wait until we can talk about this in person?" he pleaded with me but I refused to hear any of it.

"No! I never want to see you again!" I screamed and with that I hung up the phone, not wanting to hear anymore of his crap.

Fast forward two weeks, it is time to go back to the place where it all started: Sunset Beach. I knew that I would get there before he would, about three days earlier to be exact. It's one of our many traditions that the second night that we are down there we throw a dessert party on the island. Specifically at Morgan's house is where we have our festivities. It's always a good time because it is usually the first time that we are all together. It's really just a chance to catch up and start our summer from where we left it this year. Being that Victor and I were on bad terms I was definitely going to use these first three days to get a level head and then I would work it out with him. And I was sure it would all work out, that's what I was sure of. As long as I had these first three days, I was positive that we could make it work.

The way Morgan's house works is, it sits on stilts like most of the houses down there in case of hurricanes, the first level has a screened in porch and then the second level also has an open balcony. Most of the adults tended to hang out on the screened in porch where as the kids mostly hung out on the balcony. It was just the girls on the balcony sitting in the multicolored rocking chairs. By the girls I mean it was Sara, Morgan, and I. We were people watching off the balcony, which didn't happen often only because the island was so small that there weren't many people to watch. The next person we saw however is a jogger. He was young, probably around our age, and the next thing we realized was we know this guy. Victor was jogging down the road right in front of our dessert party! But how is this possible, he wasn't supposed to be here for another day or so!

And then the shouting began, "Victor! Victor!" Sara and Morgan cried in unison.

"Guys stop I don't want to see him, please stop!" I pleaded with them, this couldn't really be happening to me right now.

"Victor! Victor!" they seemed to scream even louder.

The jogger slowed to a stop, it was really him. Then the adults saw him so my mom and Aunt Laurie started shouting for him to come up as well. Why was the whole world trying to conspire against me? I didn't get it. He screamed a greeting back and decided to come up, obviously excited to see me. He got up to the balcony and said hi with such an excited innocence in his eyes. He opened his arms to where I was supposed to fit in for a hug. I didn't I walked right past him and went directly to my mother.

"Mom I'm going to the beach, don't tell anyone where I am, I have my cell phone if you need me." I told her.

"Okay? Are you alright?" She asked.

I mumbled some kind of response that was good enough that she let me go. So I walked away each step teeming with anger. I didn't know who to be the maddest at either: Victor for the whole

Jamie thing or Sara and Morgan for calling him over in the first place. I decided it didn't matter as long as I got myself out of there.

The first thing I did when I got to the pier was, I walked straight to the water and just sat by the edge. I was so angry I couldn't believe it. I decided I needed to talk to someone so I called my best friend at the time, Kyle. Luckily Kyle answered and I started ranting about the whole situation. By the end he was just as furious as I was at all three of them. I was especially glad about this that I had someone on my side; yes I was that immature at the time. By the time I hung up with Kyle, I felt a little bit better. I started pacing by the edge of the water. Then I felt a tap on my back. I turned around and low and behold it was Victor. All the anger that I thought I got out of my system came rushing back.

"What the hell do you want?" I half screamed at him, I didn't want to talk to him, I didn't want to see him, and I didn't want anything to do with him at all.

"Look Mary, calm down, I just wanted to talk to you," he said, trying to relax me. He reached out to touch my arm but I promptly shook it off.

"Don't touch me, I don't want anything to do with you!" I screamed at him, this time full on.

"Look I'm sorry that I forgot to tell you about Jamie, I didn't realize that it would be this big of a deal!" he screamed back.

"Yeah well that's your own damn fault!" I screamed even louder. By this point I noticed an elderly couple that were on a walk on the beach stop and gawk at us because we were that loud.

"Listen as long as we are being honest there is this other girl, Tara, who is really into me and she wants to go out with me but I told her I wouldn't give her an answer until I saw how things went at the beach with you." He said at a normal level this time.

"Fine! Go out with her! See if I care! It's not like I wasted a whole freaking year of my life waiting to be with you!" I screamed at him, not giving a damn about my surroundings.

"Mary don't be like this, if you don't want me to be with her then I won't I just need to know what you think." He said calmly.

"Well I don't care do what you want, I'm out of here!" And I started to walk away, and as I did I felt him grab my arm. I whipped around and like a cobra ready to spit my venom I screamed, "What do you want now!?"

"Well can I at least get a hug for the past year that we've been through together?" He asked, obviously hurt by the way that I was treating him.

"No!" I spat back at him and with that I stalked off back to the house ready to give Sara and Morgan a piece of mind. Little did I know the ramifications that would be because I never looked back when I walked away from the beach on that warm August day.

Via Morgan
Chapter Sixteen: The Hint

A few days went by of just waiting and wondering what was happening in his life. I desperately wanted to talk to him and be close to him again. I felt like we had this bond together. We were connected emotionally, or at least I was connected to him emotionally. However, I realized it was almost impossible for us to keep in touch as much as I wanted. He was five hours away, and didn't have his own cell phone. We had to rely on instant messenger.

After a few days of refusing to leave the computer screen in hopes I would not miss him, I received an IM from an unknown name. "Hey beautiful. I miss you already." I was extremely perplexed. Who was this person and why were they trying to talk to me? There was a thought in the back of my head that maybe; just maybe it was him that was trying to get in touch with me. I quickly shot down that idea in hopes not to be disappointed when it was not him.

"Who is this," I wrote him with an attitude. I don't like it when random people try to talk to me.

"Uh, its Zack," said my knight in shining armor ready to save me from a life of waiting for him. My heart had stopped beating. I hadn't been that happy in days. It was just what I needed to make it through the next few days.

The rest of the conversation is a blur. It is just like the next three weeks of my life. About 95% of all of my memory is lost from that time. We talked just about every day on AIM. Most of it was nothing important, but it was important for me. I saved every single word he ever said to me. It was the most important thing to me. Everyday we didn't speak I was on my computer rereading everything he had ever said to me. I would sit there and try to remember his face, his voice, and the way his touch felt like. It was the only way that kept me still going day after day. Even though it was hard somehow we made it through, and we were happy.

About a week and a half after we got home from the beach, I went out to dinner with my best friend from a few years before, Madeline. Madeline and I had been inseparable for about 6 years of my life. She knew a lot about me, or at least she thought she did. She was a big part of who I was then. She had in a way made me. I needed to tell her the story, because I desperately needed her approval. It was a story that was kind of ridiculous. I mean, who falls in love in four days when your just simply fourteen years old.

"Are you serious? Are you really thinking about staying with him? Morgan, you better be careful," said my concerned friend.

"Yeah, I really am thinking about it. I don't think that it will be all that hard. I think that as long as we have strong feelings for each other, we can last. Oh, and don't worry I am going to be careful. He would never hurt me. He is not like that." I said in my defense.

"No, that's not what I mean. Morgan, you are a slut. You will cheat on him. You are going to hurt him. Why don't you just end it now? It will just make it easier, so he wont hate you." Her words still ring in my head. Is this chick really telling me that I am a slut! However, I thought she was right. I thought she knew me so well. It was possible I was with Jeff for way to long and it was true. I was just a slut.

I never considered myself a slut. She was my best friend, though, so she must have just known more than I did. She was the person that knew me the most. She was the person I had looked up to for so many years. I believed every word she said about me, no matter if it was wrong or right. I had made some bad decisions with Jeff, and I had been pushed into doing more than I wanted, but I was a virgin. Yes, I was a flirt, but did that make me a slut? I guess that I thought that Jeff had made me into a boy crazed sex fiend. The contradiction there was not clear to me at that time. I was just convinced that I was a bad person and that I could not do anything right. I was screwed.

The thing was I didn't want to hurt him. I would do anything to keep him from being hurt by me. I couldn't stand for him to have to go through a hard time. What was I going to do? No matter what I did, it would it was going to be the wrong thing.

We were sitting in the movie and I just couldn't pay attention. I was just thinking about what I was going to do about my situation. All of a sudden I get a text message from the one and only Zack. "Hey. How is the movie?" He floored me. How did he know where I was? He always had great timing. For some reason, he always text me at the perfect time. It was like he knew when I needed him the most.

We talked for a minute; just until I figured out he was not a creeper. He had been looking for me, and had called Mary to find out where I was. I was impressed that he cared enough to stalk me down.

After a while of thinking I decided that I needed him to hurt me before I could hurt him. I never told him why, but I kept giving him hints on what he needed to do. He had to hurt me before I would cheat on him. I was convinced Madeline was right. I was an evil slut and wanted to hook up with everyone in the entire world. I mean, I had manipulated Zack to get with me. Even though I couldn't seem to imagine myself ever being with anyone else.

For the next few days, my idea was just to convince him how bad I actually was. He needed to know how we were not right for each other, even though my heart screamed at me after every word I typed to him. "You know. Maybe this is just too hard. Maybe you should look for another girlfriend. I don't want to hold you back. You're going to high school, and I just don't be the reason you don't have a good time. This is just too hard. You should do it. You should start looking for another girl in Pittsburgh" I said as my heart ripped in half painfully, however I thought that it was the right thing.

"Stop. You're crazy. I don't want to be with anyone else but you. I don't need anyone closer. I don't think it's that hard maybe we can just try it for a little bit longer." He said trying to fight his point. It was for the best I knew, because I could live with me being unhappy but I couldn't live with him being unhappy because of me.

The fight lasted for days. He just wouldn't let me win. I guess I shouldn't have expected he would. He was always stubborn and had to win every little fight, even if it was over the word "on." The thing was that every single time we fought I would always back down. It was never as important to me to win as it was to him, so I let him win a lot. It wasn't worth the fight. This time it was though. I was not going to let him win. I thought that I was doing the right thing. I thought I was being noble.

Finally the fight got so bad and so heated, he said, "We have to talk about this. Can I call you?" It was something that I needed. We had never talked on the phone and it was the perfect time for it. We were slipping away quickly and it was all of my fault. I was scared of losing him, but at the same time I was afraid to feel the way I did.

The phone conversation was quick and the words were nothing important, but for some reason he knew how to make me feel better. The words were not speculator and they were just simple words that if they were spoken by anyone else would not have affected me even the slightest. He said them though. He made me realize how stupid I was being. I was just scared, and at that moment I knew that I wanted to be with him. I knew I couldn't just push him away because I was afraid of hurting him. That was no way of living.

That night after the call, I was so sure of what I felt about him, I went and wrote in my journal. The very first line read "I thank God for blessing me to have met him. But yet, he is so perfect and I just wish I could be with him." I was sold on him once again. Soon, I would learn he was sold on something too.

For a reason that has now been lost with the time, we hadn't talked for a few days. For some reason I want to say he was punished for something stupid. Some thing's about that time is strangely blurry. I don't know why I was not upset for not talking to him for a few days. Maybe it was because I had just heard his voice. Sometimes with him we could talk and then it wouldn't matter if we didn't talk for a few days because I would be okay. I could hold myself over just replaying the words that he said to me. He always knew exactly what to say.

By the time he came back about three days later, everything had changed. It is strange how such a short time can change your entire life and your entire heart. He told me that he had met this really nice girl, and he was thinking of asking her out. It was the worst thing that I had ever heard anyone say to me. I had got what I wished for. He was moving on and there was nothing I could do about it.

I could feel my heart breaking with every word he said. As soon as I realized that what I was doing was not what I wanted, he listened to me! He never listened to me, so I didn't know why he chose now to start. I had to fight for him now. I cried and yelled at him to stop and just be with me. "I thought that this is what you wanted." He said, wondering what he had done wrong.

The fight went on for days. Every time we talked it was a struggle to talk about anything but that. He was trying to get me to understand, but I just couldn't. I realized that I was not good enough for him. There must be something wrong with me that he didn't want to be with me anymore. This knew girl must be skinnier, prettier, and smarter than me, I said to myself. This was my nightmare.

Finally August 20 came around, the day I will never forget. He signed on AIM. "I can't talk for long because I've been punished but I need to talk to you. We can't talk for a week but I have to tell you. I ended up asking that girl out. She is my girlfriend now." My life was crashing in front of my eyes. Two weeks before a new school year and I realized I could never be happy again. Life as I knew it was to be forever damned. He continued to say the sentence I will never forget, "We might be with other people, but we will not feel the same about them as we feel about each other."

Those were the infamous words that ended our relationship. That is not the way to end it, however. That is the way to keep a girl stringing along. When you hear those words you have mixed emotions. Part of you is torn apart knowing that he is with someone else. The very thought of him hugging some other girl was tearing me a part. However, this is the way that you make a girl feel like she's more important than the new girl. That was his way of ending it, but it makes it seem like your starting it in a way. It was the wrong way to end it.

Days went by and everything was started to feel better. I found the perfect rebound guy he got my mind off of the pain I was feeling because of Zack. However, I felt guilty. I still thought that Zack and I were technically together. I learned soon that I was very much mistaken. The days turned into weeks, and Zack had not talked to me. I checked my emails everyday, but they were always empty. My phone never rang. It became clear that it was not the same, and he did not feel the same way about me any longer. For the first time, I realized why rebounding was wrong. It made everything so much more complicated. I was missing Zack and crying myself to sleep every night, but I had to put on a happy face when I talked to the outside world. No one could understand. I was alone.

Two months passed and I finally got up the nerve to talk to him. He was online for the first time and months. I knew that I would not be able to live with myself if I didn't try to talk to him. We talked for maybe five minutes. Nothing special was discussed. We basically only did introductions. It was what I needed. I wondered what that meant and where we stood. I didn't know if we were together or not.

The complete avoidance of what we were kept me strung along for months. I assumed that everything was how we left off. I assumed that he shared feelings for me just like I still felt for him. I couldn't imagine that he could have changed his mind so quickly about me.

As the months flew by I realized they had. By December I knew that he was over me. We rarely talked, and when we did we only talked about football. However, what hurt me the most was the fact that my younger cousin Sara talked to him more than I did. I realized he was slipping out of my reach. He was gone. I wasn't ready yet though. I still had hope that one day we would rekindle our relationship.

New Years came around. It was a new year, and I wanted it to be a new start. I wanted to move on, but I couldn't without telling him everything I had in my heart. The letter ended up being about two pages long. The exact words have been lost with time. I told him exactly how I felt. I told him that he was the best thing that ever happened to me. I told him that I didn't know if life was worth living without him. I told him that I would do anything to be with him again and how I was devastated when it ended.

The whole idea of the letter was just to get it out of my system so that I could finally move on. I sent it to Mary, however, to make sure that she understood exactly how I was feeling. She read it and urged me to send it to him. She thought that it was important for him to read it. I took her advice and emailed it to him.

A few days later he read the letter and got online. He "imed" me trying to talk this whole thing out. He decided the best way to get through to me was anger. That was the day that I learned that expressing yourself was the wrong thing to do. Everything I said was wrong even my feelings. He was so upset with what I was saying. All I wanted to hear was that my feelings were justified and I was not crazy for feeling this way. However, he gave me the opposite. He belittled me by saying things that demolished my pride and broke my heart.

"Chill, we were only 15." That was the first thing that he said to me after reading the words from my heart. Fifteen years on this earth were just not enough to be able to experience love in his mind. He just didn't know how to stop there. "You were the first girl I ever went out with…I was stupid then." I was convinced that Mary could hear my heart screaming in pain 10 miles away. I just could not believe that someone I felt so strongly about could say something so painful. Immediately after saying that he said, "Why cant we just be friends?"

I wanted to die right then and there. I had never felt so uncared about in my entire life. I was telling him I loved him, and his response was that he was stupid for ever being with me. I could just see my self-esteem dropping by the moment. What was wrong with me? What did I do wrong? Why are the girls in Pittsburgh better than me? I closed my eyes and just hoped that one day that pain would stop.

September

October

November

Via Mary
Chapter Seventeen: Silence

Tara. Her name was Tara. This was the girl that Victor found to essentially replace me. He had told me about her when we were arguing at the beach. She was really into him but he was going to wait to see how I felt about it before giving her an answer. Tara was the reason that I would not hear from him for months. I didn't know this at the time; I thought it would all blow over. Tara had other plans. Plans to rip us from the seams.

But what could I do? I was angry with him for this whole Jamie thing and there was no way I was just going to "be cool" or "let it go." So we didn't talk, and we wouldn't talk and that would be okay. I would find a way to distract myself from thoughts of him. I would find a way to cope and to live my life normally and without some guy that lived more than a thousand miles away from me. This would be easy. This would be okay. I could do this. Or I could always just resort to crying myself to sleep and praying for him to call. Which you know, in times of weakness I may have done just that. But I was a girl so technically that was okay. Or so I told myself.

The truth is, I wanted him, no I needed him in my life. I didn't care how foolish it felt to be in love with someone who lived over a thousand miles away, this was my truth, my life. My heart was at stake and I wasn't willing to just let it get pulverized so easily. But just as I did in any crisis situation like this current one, I did nothing. I didn't text him, I didn't e-mail him and I sure as hell didn't call him. I wanted to give in so badly to him and to beg him to take me back but my pride got the best of me. So I played the waiting game. Nothing. My phone didn't ring. My inbox was stagnant. I was a wreck. I couldn't believe he was actually putting me through this.

What was so good about Tara anyway? I had seen pictures and trust me she wasn't all that pretty. I had talked to her on the phone before when Victor and I dated; her personality didn't seem to pop like mine did. I didn't get what was so great about her. Maybe I was just jealous, okay so I was definitely just jealous but still, what gives?? All I knew about stinkin' Tara is that I wanted her out of the picture although I feared that was my position. I guess her main advantage over me was that she lived in the same zip code so she won that fair and square. Still, more than ever, I wanted my phone to ring.

I hadn't spoken to Victor in months, he had really moved on and I had to face the certain reality that we may be over. I knew the hardest part was ahead. I had to get to a point where I could look at him and feel nothing. But just like Cory in Boy Meets World, when people asked me how I felt about it being over, I stood there with the knowledge that it really wasn't. It never could be. Our love ran too deep to be ended by someone else coming in the picture. We may be on life support, but damn it; we were still alive. I knew this simply because after four months of silence, my phone rang.

Via Morgan
Chapter Eighteen: But, Maybe?

My whole life had just gone down the drain. Everything was over, and I was alone. Being alone was always something that I was petrified of. I always felt that you had to have someone in your life, okay you had have a guy in your life, to be happy. You had to be romantically involved to have a fulfilling life. So, I was just doomed to be unhappy.

Jeff was gone. I ignored him for as long as I could hoping to prolong the anger that was inevitably about to be thrown at me. Finally, I gave in. About a week after I arrived home from the beach, I heard the heated voice on the other end of the telephone. "How could you do this to me? How could you cheat on me? We were not over."

"Seriously, dude? I broke up with you months ago. It's over. Get over it. I didn't do anything to you. We are over, and I found someone who actually cares about me." I yelled back right before hanging up the phone.

The scene from so many months before was haunting me in February of 2006. Why did I have to get rid of him? I should have just kept him around a little longer. There I was empty, and all alone. Where was I supposed to go next?

I didn't know how I was supposed to move on. I didn't know where to start. My heart was shattered into millions of pieces, and I didn't have a clue of where to start to put the puzzle back together. I made the decision I believed to be the best. I wasn't going to try to fix myself, but I was just going to try to live my life.

The first few months after the disastrous ending, all I did was cry. I began separating my life from my feelings, just so that the tears wouldn't be constantly falling. I tried to live the most normal life without feeling anything, because I knew if I felt anything I would feel the pain of losing him. He was the best thing that ever happened to me but also the worst.

I started to analyze everything that I saw and everything around me. I was just looking for something to prove to me that I wasn't broken. I just needed something to prove to me that we weren't over. I just needed it be a bad dream that I just had to wake up from. I found myself looking everywhere for signs, but it wasn't too hard because they were everywhere. Everywhere I looked, was Pittsburgh. The horrid city that was the cause of all my pain followed me where ever I turned. It made it so hard to forget him when everywhere I looked was something that reminds me of him. I so wished that I could just get on a plane and fly somewhere where the people had never heard of Sunset Beach or Pittsburgh, but being a 15 year old girl that kind of made it difficult to do.

To make it even worse it was NFL playoff season. The twelve teams were fighting to the death in hopes of being one of those two teams to make it to Detroit, where the Super bowl would be held. The Baltimore Ravens, unfortunately, were not one of those teams, considering they finished the season with a devastating record of 6-10. I was forced to watch and cheer for other teams to get to that one coveted game. One team that was in the running was the Pittsburgh Steelers.

I watched every game hoping that they would be blown away, but each time they were the ones that were being successful. It killed me to watch each game, but at the same time, I was relieved that he was at least happy. Finally, the news spread around the country. The Pittsburgh Steelers were headed to the Super bowl. When was it going to be?

The date of the Super bowl landed exactly six months after we first kissed. This was my worst nightmare. I couldn't escape my life that day. I knew that it would be a bad day originally knowing that I had to remember that just six months before was the best time of my life, and now it was destroyed. But, knowing that I had to watch the biggest reminder of him tore apart my heart once again. It made it impossible to get away from him. The whole year was filled with moments just like these which made it impossible to forget him and impossible to get over him.

There was always a thought in my mind that he would change his mind. I knew that we had something special and one day he would realize it. I was just waiting for that time to come. There was one flaw in my idea. We never talked. How was he supposed to love me again if he didn't even know me?

I tried my best to talk to him as much as I could. Each time I would get one of two different Zacks. There was the Zack that talked to me that fateful night when he told me things were over. That was the Zack that was apathetic to me. He wanted nothing to do with me, not even to be my friend. The other Zack was the Zack that I knew at the beach. He was flirty, friendly, and easy to talk to. He was open to being my friend and was trying to get that to happen. I knew I had to walk on eggshells whenever I attempted to talk to him because I never knew which one I would get. Looking back I just wish he had been one solid person. I wish he had been the apathetic Zack, because that way I could have realized that it was over.

With the two Zacks, I could dream that he still wanted to be with me too. There were dreams, though. Just about every week I would have a dream about the two of us. I confused the idea of dream and reality. I was convinced that we were meant to be and that it would be happen one day. I couldn't accept that it wouldn't. If things could change so quickly, then they surely could switch back just as quickly.

Before I could blink, it was August again. Nothing had

changed. I was desperately in love with Zack, praying that this would be the time that he would change his mind. For a whole week before the beach I couldn't eat, sleep, or even breathe, I was so nervous. I had to be perfect for him. I just had to be exactly what he wanted so that I could win him back. I just wasn't sure if I could ever connect the puzzle pieces of my heart without him. He made it impossible to put it back together because he had the last piece of my heart. It didn't matter if I wasn't being myself; because I was being what he wanted and that is all that mattered. He was more important to me than I was to me. I would do anything to have him offer that piece back to me.

We talked the night before. He was as nervous as I was. "Is everything going to be okay with us? I don't want things to be awkward. We can be friends, right?" In my mind this was perfect. The first step to relationships was friendship. This could work. It just had to work. I didn't think I could be okay if it didn't.

The first full day at the beach I woke up early frantically trying to make myself look perfect. I tried on every bathing suit I owned seeing a flaw in myself that just wouldn't cut it. I brushed my hair made it look good just to immediately throw it up into a ponytail, but then repeated the process over and over again. I contemplated putting on makeup, but then realized it would just wash off in the ocean. I had never been so nervous to see anyone in my life. What was going to happen? Were my dreams going to come true?

I walked onto the beach over the same bridge that had been stepped over just one year before. I scanned the horizon hoping to see that red and white striped umbrella, but it was not to be found. He wasn't there. A wave of relief came over me, until I saw three people walking towards me. It was Pittsburgh. Warm hellos and hugs were given to all, but I stood receiving none. I knew that this was not the year. I knew that this week was going to be worse than spending a lifetime in hell.

The rest of the week was a drama filled blur. Mary, Victor,

Morgan and Zack, AHH. Panic attacks, tears, and anger were the definition of Sunset Beach that week. Nothing was going right and we just couldn't fix it. I cannot speak for the boys, but for the girls: we left devastated. The perfect week we had been planning for 51 weeks was shattered. My week ended so badly that I refused to say goodbye to him. I left the beach on that Friday so bitterly upset that my mom had to take me kayaking for an hour so I wouldn't punch someone.

I left the beach that year knowing that I had to find a way to put the pieces of my heart back together. I realized that Zack was not going to do it for me, not anytime soon at least. There was still about three-fourths of my brain that knew that one day soon it would happen. I just had to wait for that time to come.

Just a few days later, we talked probably more than we talked in the whole time at that wonderful island. We both apologized. It didn't end up the way we had both wanted it to. We were expecting closure, but in fact we went even further back in our progress. We were not friends. It was just too soon and the wounds were just too fresh. Things ended just too brutally and things were handled in the wrong way, on both parts. We were sorry, but it didn't make things okay.

The next year we were silent, until one fateful day. That day I stumbled upon his profile. I read exactly what I prayed every night wouldn't happen. There was another girl in there. We had been over for over a year, but I still felt like I had a right to have him to myself. I know it sounds crazy, but no matter what he said, I couldn't get my heart back from his possession. I felt cheated, and obviously devastated. I closed the Internet window quickly hoping that it really didn't happen. I was just praying that I read it wrong. I sat at my desk shaking. I was terrified that I truly did see it. I sat there; head in hands for ten minutes trying to figure out my next move. I finally decided I had to look again. I opened it up and read every single word and analyzed it. Then I saw it, "Met the Coolest Girl Tuesday." This had really just happened. I ran to my room unable to breathe. I managed to reach for my phone and text Mary "Look at his profile."

She freaked out. She was completely shocked by what she just saw. "Is he serious? Who does that? Whatever it's his life if he wants to be weird so be it." She saw my pain, and knew I was hurting bad. What was I supposed to do next? I had no idea. As soon as the immediate shock and pain subsided, I realized who advertises that. Who was this guy, because I sure as hell had no idea who he had become. He was not the person that I knew anymore. I realized I might never know him again.

"Met the Coolest Girl Tuesday" became his life. She consumed him, and I had no chance of coming back into his life. I was not going to give up. He would still be the one that got away no matter what. He was, as Mary once said, "my addiction." He was one of the only positive things in my life and I refused to let it go. I just thought that it was not time yet. Maybe, he was just always going to be something special to me. Maybe he was just going to be someone that I would compare every last person that came in and out of my life to. Needless to say, some cool girl from Tuesday was not going to change what I felt.

Six months came around and the beach was here once again. This was the second year I had seen him since those five perfect days. I knew that they were together, and I did not expect a thing. I didn't even know if there was anything there for him anymore. Maybe he was just a memory, an awful memory, I just couldn't shake. I wanted desperately to be his friend. Why did it seem like it was impossible? No matter how hard I tried, it felt like it could never happen. Probably because as soon as I walked over that wooden bridge walk way to the beach I saw that red and white striped umbrella. That stupid umbrella that should have meant nothing to me, made me remember who he was that week twenty-four months before. I was rushed by emotion and was once again not sure if I could do this. I tried to figure out how to shut down those thoughts and even worse those feelings. What was it about that beach? What was the Kindred Spirit trying to tell me? I guess that I always had a feeling in my gut that Kindred Spirit still had plans for us.

I swallowed my fears and stepped onto that beach. I thought that I could just avoid him for a week. A few hours killed that dream. We said hello and that was it for a few days. Something was different about this week. Mary had a friend down at the beach this week. It was never just the three of us. We were paired off, which was fine except that sometimes I was left alone. I had to venture off to the unknown territory of Pittsburgh. We refer the sections of the beach by the people that occupy it. We have Baltimore, Pittsburgh, Canada to refer to all the way up the beach, and West Virginia to refer to down the beach or the place no one wanted to go. Well anyway, I had to go to a territory of Pittsburgh that was frightening and where I was not sure if I was welcomed. The more time I spent with them the more comfortable I got. The whole group was welcoming, eventually. Well, Megan and Kate were always the best. They would always be there for me no matter what. That I knew. They were not the ones that I had to worry about. They were the best kind of friends. They were the friends that would last no matter how far away they were, how little we talked, or how little we really had in common. They were perfect. It was Zack that I had to worry about.

By the end of the week something strange had happen, we were actually becoming friends. I was beginning to trust him and value his opinion. He had opened up to me about this "Met the Coolest Girl Tuesday." They were fighting, and they were thinking about breaking up. "Perfect," I thought. "I'll just be the one that picks up the pieces when he is all upset about her after they break up." I never expect what to happen to happen though.

He did not have a phone, and he was desperate to talk to her. I did something that I probably should not have done. Being the newfound friend I did what I would do to any other friend, I offered for him to take my phone for the night to talk to her. He accepted, which I never expected him to. Why was I so stupid? Why me of all people? He took the phone on Thursday night and talked to her all night and all day Friday at the beach. The problem was that on Friday I held the phone and let him know when she texted him back. Between every text that was sent, I read the conversation. It was probably not the right thing to do but shit it was on my phone. What I saw was something I had been hoping for. She broke up with him over text message on my phone.

"This girl must not know who I am," I thought. I was so sure that I was so special to him when it is clear that I wasn't, but I refused to hear that then. I was convinced that my devious plan was just falling right into place. He was so close to being mine. I could just feel it in my gut. We were finally exactly what I wanted. We were friends. We were close friends that could actually talk to one another. Maybe this would last. I was overcome by excitement, being Zack's friend was what I had been hoping for, for quite a long time.

I went home thinking that this friendship would last. I thought that we would continue to talk as soon as we got home. I was mistaken. As soon as I stepped foot back into Baltimore, it was like nothing had happened. The beach had lied to me. The Kindred Spirit was no longer there to protect me and to watch over us. We fell a part and went another year in silence. I wondered how the vicious cycle would end. I wondered when the madness would stop, and if this friendship was ever possible. I have had many conversations with Zack over the years about why we could never be friends. Every time he would answer, "IDK, its just weird. We were together and then it just ended."

I have never been a witty person. I have always been something that cannot think quickly. I need to sit and think about it before I can answer. So needless to say each time he said it to me I could never get the next question out in time. Why could he be a friend with "Met the Coolest Girl Tuesday" and not me? What was the difference between the two of us? I guess I would just never know. It would always just be a thought that will haunt me.

The next year passed and a week at Sunset had flown by. Nothing had changed. We were still in the same place. We had made no progress nor did we take steps back. We were at a stale mate. We were not the way we had been the year before, but we were no the way we were that first year after the beach. We were awkward, and we avoided each other. It was like we were both scared to get close to each other. It is something I don't understand. What did he have to lose? He was the one that didn't care about me, so why didn't he want to be my friend. I always knew that there was something that I didn't know. There would always be thing that I would never understand about him and our story. Maybe this was what we were meant to be. Maybe, we were meant to be an awkward acquaintanceship was our destiny. I was convinced that it was just too hard for us to put the past behind us. But what was holding him back?

Via Mary
Chapter Nineteen: Rebirth

"Hello?" I said, my voice shaking just like the rest of my body.
"Hey Mary, it's Victor." He said simply.

We started to talk and I'm not going to lie it was very awkward at first. But sooner than I would come to realize, we were laughing and chatting. Then his tone shifted to a more serious one. He started to talk about Tara. It had been four months since we had spoken so I didn't even know if she was still in the picture. As he kept talking about her I realized that they were still together and they were very happy. I was crushed. He said he still loved me as a friend. I started to cry. I was nowhere near over him and yet here he was completely moved on. What was I going to do? This was my life. I could have sworn this would just blow over. He was in the middle of saying something when his voice momentarily cut out. He told me to hold on, someone was on the other line. His voice came back and then he said the words that nearly killed me.

"Mary, I'm sorry, I have to go, Tara is on the other line." And with that, the line was dead.

He had done it. He had chosen her over me. I was officially broken. I sat there with the phone on my ear for a few more moments, begging for his voice to come back on the line, waiting for him to tell me that he was kidding and that he still loved me. He didn't. He was gone. The hollow existence that I had lived for the past few months came crashing down and all that was left was nothing.

In the months to come there was very little communication between us. He was consumed in his new life with Tara and I was left to pick up the pieces of my own existence. Don't get me wrong, we still talked here and there and called ourselves friends. But really, we weren't. We couldn't be because I was so consumed with getting him back. All I wanted was to be with him.

And then finally the day came where I got another phone call. It was Victor. I figured it would just be a routine checking in, seeing how I was and the like.

"Mary I need to tell you something." He said very seriously.

"Okay, what is it? Is everything okay?" I asked just as seriously as he was.

"I don't love Tara; I'm still in love with you." He said.

My heart soared. I couldn't believe that this was actually happening. He really did still love me. All of the silence had really meant nothing. We were going to be okay after all.

Things were a little shaky at first; I wasn't sure what to do or if I was saying the right thing at the right time. I was nervous all over again just like an elementary school girl with a crush on the hot shot 4th grader. I only wanted to impress. The biggest question still remained unanswered, when would we start saying, "I love you" again, or would we even still say it? I decided not to go there quite yet. Instead, we just talked and got to know each other again.

It was interesting to notice all of the little subtleties in his personality that I had missed over the time that we didn't talk. Like the way his voice would get softer when he would say affectionate things to me. It was easy to fall in love with him again. Well, I never really fell out of love, but it felt good to reconnect. I was so happy to just be able to talk to him freely again. I didn't have to worry about what Tara would hear; I didn't have to worry about whether or not I was saying too much. I could just be me and that was okay with him. Everything was going great, and we were even going to see each other at the beach soon. This was nothing short of perfect.

Via Morgan
Chapter Twenty: "Broken Girl Breaking Out of the Nest into the Whole World."

I woke up to the voice of one of the adults saying, "You better put sun tan lotion on or come under the tent. That Sunset Beach Sun has killed your back." I opened my eyes and realized. It was four years since I had met Zack and I was lying on my stomach trying to cover up the white skin that has replaced a tan since I had slaved over a job I love for the past year. I was two weeks away from moving into a new apartment. I was eighteen years old and I was getting ready to break away and go to my dream college, University of Maryland. I just couldn't believe that high school was over, and that four whole years have passed since I had met Zack. I took a look out to the ocean and remembered everything from the past four years.

After Zack and I were over, I was devastated. I didn't sleep for months. I could not even look at another guy for a year and a half. It just always seemed too soon. After many failed tried attempts at an escape from the pain he caused me, I finally found one that fit perfectly. I returned to an old friend: anorexia.

For about seven years of my life, on and off, anorexia helped me to numb every kind of pain I could have imagined. That was perfect for me. I wouldn't let myself eat because I wasn't worthy enough for the food. Then it got to the point that I was so tired and without energy that I couldn't feel a thing even if I wanted to. I didn't have to be upset anymore. For three years I lived by just going through the motions of life, because I was too tired and upset to live it. It was just what I needed. I was afraid of being hurt again, and was not willing to take the chance.

However since I am a "slut," like my old best friend Madeline once said to me, I could not live without a guy in my life. I went though several different meaningless relationships. The only time I would allow myself into a relationship was if I knew that I would feel nothing for them. I dated the needy, the druggies, the apathetic surfers, and the unattractive. It was the only way that I could. I could not imagine being alone, but couldn't be emotionally attached to anyone else.

Life was spiraling out of control at a rapid speed, and I felt like there was nothing I could do. For a long time I was okay with that life. I didn't need to be anything more or less. I was happy being unhappy. It was the perfect life for me to have. My perfect unhappy life last about a year and a half until it got so out of control I could not bare to be that way for another minute.

My sister left for college. My last connect holding my unhappy life together was gone. My best friend, my protector, my annoying late night call to rub her back, was leaving for good. Everyone told me it was not for good but I soon realized it was true. Our relationship would be forever tainted. It would never be the same way that I need it to be. I lost my best friend. Nothing in life was the same after that dreadful day she left. School, sports, dance, friends, and my house were different now. My life was unbearable.

My old friend Anorexia became my best friend instead of Ashley. She took over my life. She was my life. Every thought, dream, word, and even breath became how to avoid eating a meal, and I was successful. I became an apathetic soul who cared about nothing but food, and I was so happy about that.

In about two months I ended up losing thirty pounds. I would eat one meal a day and exercise for about four hours a day. Five days a week I had two-hour field hockey practice of running and agility. Then at least three days a week I would have dance for two to four hours directly after hockey practice. Then on the weekends I would rush to Brick Bodies, the gym we belonged to. I was out of control, and liking it. I had the classical eating disorder symptoms of demanding control and perfection. I was dying for approval from everyone around me so I knew how to play them, and I knew who to eat around and whom I could manage to not eat around. I began to spend a lot of time with this group of 5 girls from my high school. They were not necessarily great friends originally, but they were gullible. They fell for whatever lie I could dish out to avoiding eating, and they were fine with it. My tricks were brilliant. I knew that if I ate fatty foods no one would expect a thing. I made sure that certain people would see me eating that bag a chips, but little did they know that was the only thing I was going to eat for the day.

I brushed it off as a problem that everyone goes through and kept telling myself it was nothing to worry about. You look great. You need to be a little skinnier, though. What is the problem? You just are too busy to eat. It is not a problem. I had myself convinced I was fine. When people came up to me and said ever so rudely "Do you eat?" I would simply reply, "Who has time to eat?" I was so convinced that I was okay.

Then my sister left for college. My last connect holding my unhappy life together was gone. My best friend, my protector, my annoying late night call to rub her back, was leaving for good. Everyone told me it was not for good, but I soon realized it was true. Our relationship would be forever tainted. It would never be the same way that I need it to be. I had lost my best friend. Nothing in life was the same after that dreadful day she left. School, sports, dance, friends, and my house were different now. My life was unbearable.

My old friend anorexia became my best friend. She took over my life. She was my life. Every thought, dream, word, and even breath became how to avoid eating a meal, and I was successful. I became an apathetic soul who cared about nothing but food, and I was so happy about that. In about two months I ended up losing thirty pounds. I would eat one meal a day and exercise for about four hours a day. I was out of control, and liking it.

I brushed it off as a problem that everyone goes through and kept telling myself it was nothing to worry about. You look great. You need to be a little skinnier, though. What is the problem? You just are too busy to eat. It is not a problem. I had myself convinced I was fine. When people came up to me and said ever so rudely "Do you eat?" I would simply reply, "Who has time to eat?" I was so convinced that I was okay.

In my mind I made a miraculous recovery over night. My mind convinced me that I was fine and I had no need to worry any longer. However, I kept living my life the same way, numb to the world, and obsessed with food and exercise. Things got worse, though. Life got harder by fights with friends, and my cousin Nick almost dying in a car accident. I didn't know how to fix everything around me from getting worse than they already were. How could things get any worse, but a better question was how could they possibly get any better?

I started going to church with Mary. I started to get involved with the people at my church. I fell in love with every single person I met and loved their openness and their loving hearts. I got lured into an event called NCYC, National Catholic Youth Conference. At first, I was leery about going to an event with 20,000 "Jesus freaks", like I totally did not think that would be fun at all. I wanted to give it a chance though.

The experience turned my life around. That was the weekend that I admitted that I had a problem. I admitted to a friend about my eating disorder for the first time. The many different inspirational speakers spoke directly to my heart. It was like I was the only person in the room, and they were speaking directly at me. They told me what to do, and how to do it. They told me not to be afraid and as long as you try it will be fine, as long as you have God on your side.

After that weekend, I was determined to get better. I tried the next two months to do it on my own but ended up getting worse. My body at that point was so exhausted from years of torture I could barely dance. Something that had been so important to me for such a long time was painful and I would go home and crash for days. My school work suffered, and I worried I would not be able to make it into college. That is it. I can't do this any longer. I need more help.

I went to Mary for help. She was my best friend and she had to be able to help me. I was petrified at her reaction. Her reaction after I told her was something resembled apathy. She seemed to brush it off like it really wasn't that big deal. I was devastated. I had just got the nerve to tell her this and she was belittling this? I shrugged off the comment pretending it didn't faze me. She promised to help me. I made her promise not to tell anyone especially Ashley. Ashley had dealt with friends with eating disorders, and I had watched her cry over it for months. Plus, she didn't need the stress her first semester in college. I was feeling like I was making progress, and was proud of myself.

I guess it wasn't enough though. I soon discovered my best friend had pulled the covering from my secret best friend. The list of people who knew about my eating disorder quickly amount to hundreds, or at least that's what it felt like. Mary and Sara's moms both knew, okay that was okay. Our youth minister found out, okay I guess that's okay. Everyone I knew was hinting at it, trying to get me to confess. I was being surrounded. Dance teachers, grandparents, aunts, uncles, cousins, friends, and even parents of friends. AHHH! When was this going to end? Finally, the worst was discovered. She told Ashley.

Mary had broken my trust. I did not know if I could ever trust her again. How did she have any right to spread the secret corners of my life? I hold her secrets deep down inside of me to this day, so why couldn't she do the same? I saw everything getting worse, and I saw myself eating less. I knew that this would be the end of a four-year friendship. I was being attacked constantly not only by people fishing for information but also by Mary herself.

After a few interventions I ended up telling my mother. She shipped me off to the Sheppard Pratt's outpatient program. Sheppard Pratt is a mental health institution in Towson, Maryland. Whenever any one heard I was going there it was a big turn off to everyone. "Ew. You must be really crazy. I don't really want to be around you any more." I do not care if that makes me look crazy because it was the best decision of my life.

I was in outpatient treatment for a year and a half. I saw a psychologist, psychiatrist, and a nutritionist. I spend most of my time at Sheppard Pratt. I was there two to three times a week every week. I finally began to make progress after my psychologist decided to place me into a group therapy. There I met my best friends that I am confident that I will know for the rest of my life. They understood me, and they didn't judge me. They were finally the people that pulled me out of my shell.

I walked into the first group thinking that these girls would be vindictive, manipulating, judgmental snobs. They would not understand me, and they would sure believe that I was not welcome there. I was so incredibly self-conscious walking in. I was not the smallest of girls, and I knew that. They would just see me as the fat girl. I sat down and we started talking. "The Bulimics" held the conversation that day. "The Bulimics" consisted of four original girls Kara, Tiffany, Stephanie, and Katie, and of course Ellie soon joined along with various others that came in and out. They were outspoken, insecure, and down to earth but at the same time they were open about how much their lives sucked. I admired these girls, and wanted to be like them. "The Anorexics" were quiet and withdrawn. At least we were the first day. It was originally just a girl named Emily and I. I felt like I was outnumbered and didn't belong until the next week when we evened out the score a little by adding Lizzie to our team.

There was something that instantly connected us together. We instantly trusted each other, and knew that this was the right thing for us to do. As the weeks flew by our therapist actually had to yell at us every week for talking too much. We just couldn't get it all out in just the hour and fifteen minutes. We began to congregate outside of the elevator for at least an hour after every session. They were becoming people I depended on.

I had things in common with all of the girls. Katie and Lizzie went to all girl schools like mine. Catholic all girls schools try to form a uniform kind of person, so we were all the same in we were in our own ways rebelling from that. Tiffany danced. Kara was artistic and creative. Emily and Ellie were quiet just like I was. Then there was Stephanie. Stephanie and I originally had nothing in common. I thought that she was the one person I really would never connect with. However, as the weeks went by I realized that we had something special; we were always going through the same thing at the same time. Stephanie became my rock, and she became the idea that what I was going through was not just happening to me. Group would not have been so great if any of these girls were not there.

The amount of us that there were was rarely eight. About half of us have at one point, sometimes even a couple points, were in higher care. They either went Inpatient, or PHP, which was inpatient without sleeping there. As one of the ones that never left, it was hard seeing everyone go back and forth but we knew it was for the best. As soon as they came back it just felt like they were never gone. The bond was never in the slightest bit broken. That's when I knew that no matter how much time had past we would always be close.

We forced each other to deal with our issues. Deep darkest secrets would come flying out of someone just about every week. Some secrets were horrific stories from the past, but most were just problems for everyday life. We all had our separate issues. In the group of eight we had problems ranging from sexuality, drugs and alcohol, death, to overall family issues. We all had one problem, one secret, in common; we had eating disorders.

For the first time in years, I was faced with the issue of Zack. I finally realized that what I had with Zack was not all that rare. It happened everyday, and it was nothing to be hung up on for that long of a time. I realized that I had the strength to get over him and any other struggles inside of myself. I did not have to have a guy, or anyone for that matter, to help me. I needed to do it myself. I needed to figure it out for myself. I had the power to fix everything in my life, and I had the girls from group to support my every move.

I realized they would never go away. Honestly, I never wanted them too. I knew that life would be easier if they were around. They were the people that knew me better than anyone. I would be there for them no matter what, and they would do the same for me. They were the best people I had ever met, and I believe that joining the group was the best decision I ever made. I could see things changing. I could see things getting better. I realized that as long as they were in my life I could get better.

Slowly but surely everything started to get better. My friendships got stronger, my family life improved, my work life got better, and I started to feel something strange, happiness. Not everything was perfect though.

The one thing that was still a mess was my love life. I still had to have a guy in my life, but I did still not trust enough to get it. I continued to roam around with useless and not worth my time guys. It was the one lesson I couldn't teach myself. I had no idea how to be stable on my own. I decided to put that fact behind me and to just give into my old ways of being "slutty." I was not ready to settle and that was okay.

I had the perfect relationship, Danny. He was there when I needed someone, and very distant when I didn't need him. He was that late night call when I was upset, and needed to get out. He knew me but yet I don't know how because real conversations were not that frequent. He was the one that made me feel immediately better but in the long run made me feel worse. He was my realization that I was not getting better with trust because I was really getting worse. Danny was the longest standing throwaway guy. He lasted for almost two years. He was the closest thing to a relationship I had, even though in other people's minds he would be the furthest.

After nearly two years, my relationship with Danny came to a crashing end. It was like hitting a wall at 60 miles per hour. We spent the best night together and for the first time I saw the real side to him. That night I gave myself to him. The relationship was finally beginning to look like it was no longer just two people using each other. It was beginning to look like two friends. The next day he ended it. "I want nothing to do with you anymore." I can still hear his voice when he said it. He finally had gotten what he really wanted, and he didn't need me anymore.

For the next two days, I was devastated. I didn't know how I let him get close to my heart. I had just started trusting him and he chose to end it. I didn't know how I would trust anyone ever again. I needed someone knew, though. I needed another guy I could use and not feel for. I had no idea where to find him though.

The next day was Christmas Eve, and I had to work at Panera Bread. I went to work and it was slow. No one ever goes anywhere on Christmas Eve, not even Panera. My bad mood had final lifted and I was in the mood for a good time. I was in the mood for another guy. I was extra flirty all night because I get flirty when I am in a good mood. The closest guy to me had a girlfriend so that was not very acceptable, so I had to walk down to the sandwich line to flirt. The sandwich line was full of Hispanics. They were the only ones that didn't take off work for a holiday. They were all great guys that I had been very good friends with for a long time. However, I only saw them as friends.

The one I knew the longest, the one, which knew my sister, Pablo. He was a jokester. He was always poking fun of everyone. I always thought that it was out of disliking but I soon realized it was out of respect. We were similar in that way we were always making remarks that tip toed around the border of rudeness. He was also one of the ones that spoke the least English. There was always a language barrier between us but we still talked and flirted often. He was a sweet guy and I knew he couldn't hurt a fly.

We were talking all night but he came up to me while I was cleaning something and said to me, "Where is my present?"

"What are you talking about Pablo?" He repeated himself. "Oh Navidad? I got you me." I said as I gave him the eye and jiggled my body a little. I knew I had him.

"All I want is one kiss." He said with the cutest Spanish accent.

I did not believe him. I thought that this was just another one of his jokes. I didn't believe that he would actually be interested in me. I didn't know how old he was but I knew he was a significant amount older than me. He was a grown man and I was just a teenager. I was just planning on playing with him. "I don't know, Pablo, maybe later in the walk-in." I walked away thinking nothing would happen and it was just going to be another person I flirt with.

I walked back to my station at the front of the store. I stood there for an hour or so waiting for anyone to walk through the door. Finally, I got sick of it and decided to walk in the back and get ready to close down the store. I walked into the walk-in fridge and started collecting the things I needed. All of a sudden, in walked Pablo. He looked at me, pulled me in close, and started kissing me.

The kiss didn't last too long, but there was something about it that intrigued me. There was something different that I needed to investigate. The kissing continued for a week until New Years Eve came around. I knew that that might be the last time we could kiss for a while, because our schedule was opposite. I found myself upset that I could possibly not see him for a few weeks. That was when I realized that he was more than just a rebound. There were automatically feelings involved. There was something about Pablo that made me get over my phobia of feelings.

Flash forward eight months, and I am desperately in love. Pablo has become the guy of my dreams, my knight in shining armor. He forced me to trust him, and made it so easy to love him. He became my best friend and helped me to be the happiest I have ever been.

The thing that means the most to me is he was the one person that pushed me to believe in myself. He was the person made me look at myself and be happy with what I see. I strongly believe that because of him I am no longer in treatment for an eating disorder. He thinks that I am perfect the way that I am and refuses to think to think that I could possibly ever be any better than I already. He pushed me into believing that for myself.

I must say that I've been waiting for a long time for a guy as great as Pablo. He even supported this "book of memories." He is the guy of my dreams. I would not be where I am today if it was not for him. I am so thankful that I have him in my life. I am also thankful for the paths that lead me to him.

Pablo taught me a lot. We were together for a very long time and most of that time was wonderful. He began to control my life. I had learned four years earlier that that was not okay because of Jeff. I left Pablo accepting the fact that he was amazing for me and would never do anything bad to me.

Secrets began to flood out from our relationship and I was no longer perfect. My past addictions came flooding back. I had once again depended on someone to make me feel okay about myself. This time I learned to do it on my own. I needed to make myself feel good about myself. I cannot say that I was alone, though. I had wonderful friends to put me back in my place and support me on my road back to being the perfect person I was. I had old friends like Mary to be able to deal with the past, but I also had wonderful new friends to stay up with me at night when I was upset and watch me to make sure I don't slip. My new friends were my roommates Cam, a twenty year old from Ulney, Maryland, and Lara, also twenty from Northern New Jersey. They were the perfect girls who understood me and would be there. I also found this perfect guy named, Nhomer. He became one of the best friends I had ever had. He stayed up with me at night for hours and made me laugh. These four friends are the reason why I can stand tall by myself, when I am single, and be confident that I am okay being me.

For the first time in my life, I can honestly say I am happy. It is not a temporary bliss, like what it was with Zack, but a permanent happiness where I am happy being myself. Everything that has happened in the past four years will stay with me forever, but it is now behind me. The only thing I can hope for is to continue my road to becoming Zack's friend.

Via Mary
Chapter Twenty-One: New Ground

A few months had passed and it was getting around that time for us to go back down to the beach. Excited about seeing Victor again, I called him to talk about it. We started off with the usual light banter about this and that. Then he told me the news that I never expected nor wanted to hear. His grandmother wasn't inviting him and Cece back down to the beach this year. (Apparently she thought they were bored and didn't have fun when they came down.) What was I going to do without him? Now that I knew Sunset Beach with him, it was hard to ever imagine it without him. This couldn't really be happening; this was just another one of his jokes. It had to be. There was no way I could go to that place without him. I refused to believe that he wouldn't be there. This would have been our third summer together. And it would have been the first summer we spent together after the big fight.

In short, I panicked. When I got down to the beach that year, I looked for him everywhere. Hoping that it was all just a cruel joke. But he was nowhere to be found. There was a certain emptiness to the trip. Everyone was there except for him. We did all the same things, in the same order, at the same places. But it felt different like something was missing. I knew it was him. I found it hard to enjoy myself without him. I didn't want to dwell on it though, he wouldn't like that and I certainly wasn't going to be that dependent.

So for once I decided to actually take a break and relax. Who knew it could actually feel good to not go a million miles per hour all the time? I took the time to reconnect with my good old friend Mr. Journal. I wrote all sorts of things, poetry, random thoughts, little stories, and I even doodled my thoughts away. Some days I didn't even bother to go to the beach, instead I just stayed at home by myself and let the sweet South Carolina day take me away. I got lost in thought over nothing in particular. I enjoyed the solitude, something I rarely ever had. I let the world slow down, and more importantly, I let myself slow down with it.

The others questioned my newfound solitude, but I just shrugged it off. I was going to do what made me happy. To be honest, I thought about Victor a lot. It was so strange to be in the place that we met, yet not have him with me. I felt like this vacation though I was having fun at times, I was mostly just going through the motions. I missed him. Over the past two years he had become such a part of me. Luckily he had a cell phone by then so we were able to talk at night. I told him of how I missed him, and he made fun of me for it. (Apparently I take things personally a lot so I'm an easy target.) Every time we talked it lifted my spirits and it motivated me to make the best of my time in the place that my grandfather had worked so hard to provide for my family.

To be honest, I think that was other huge thing on my mind: my grandfather. He is someone that I loved so much and to be back in the place that he provided always created a heightened awareness of his absence, and it hurt. My grandfather was a man of much dignity and character. In the eleven years that I knew him I had learned more than a classroom could ever teach me. He believed in me before I even gave him reason to. In fact, my grandmother told me that before he passed away, my grandfather said, "That Mary, she's going places." How could he say that? I was so young. But he had such an amazing faith and love for his grandchildren that no one else could match.

Sometimes when I was home alone, I would just pace around the different rooms. I would admire them for what they were, always knowing that my grandfather decorated each and every one himself. Victor reminded me a lot of my grandfather. From the calm tones he used when talking to me, to his generally supportive nature. I think that's why it was so easy to fall in love with him.

After a few days of moping around I finally decided to get back on my feet and really enjoy this vacation. Surprisingly, I had a blast with the girls, and I got to know the Pittsburgh kids: Megan, Katie, Bubby (Bobby), and of course Zack better too. Megan and Katie fit right in with Morgan, Sara, and I. In fact the Kindred Spirit on Sunset Island seemed to have had worked its magic on Megan too. Katie and Sara became really good friends, which of course was awesome to see. And Bubby, well he was just hilarious. Even the adults got along nicely. The only person that was missing was Victor, but this would be okay, I would be okay.

Little did I know the summer of the fight would be the last vacation that I would spend with Victor. In the next year to come his grandmother yet again didn't invite him down. But we were still going strong. The big question still remained, when I would see him again? It was wearing on both of us. All we wanted was to be together, yet this was a feat that seemed impossible to meet. The vacation of the fight would also foreshadow the end of other relationships as well.

Via Morgan
Chapter Twenty-Two: Unsupportive

As the fourth year came around, I was sure that Zack meant nothing to me. I was "in love" with this wonderful guy that was perfect for me. Zack was just a part of the past. He meant nothing to me, or at least I thought he didn't. I was so into my boyfriend Pablo, and I thought that no one could be better for me than him. Zack was just the past. I never loved him. It was only an infatuation.

In the middle of the week, my wonderful and perfect guy stopped being so wonderful. He stopped talking to me and decided to hang out with my best friend instead of speaking to me. I was devastated and frustrated. The people that were there for me during this time of confusion were my beach people, including those from Pittsburgh.

The little game of "we are friends, wait no were not" was actively being played between Zack and I. We still had no idea how to speak to each other. We did not know the boarders. We had no idea what we were or what we would become in the future. I got the strange feeling that we would be like this forever. We were doomed to this life in Purgatory.

It was very similar to the year before. I was fighting with Pablo just like he had been fighting with "Met the Coolest Girl Tuesday." He was nice and just like always, knew exactly what to say. He could put a smile on my face even when I wanted to cry. For example, the night of the ice cream social, Pablo and I had an awful fight. He, and honestly all the others, were there for me. The Pittsburgh-Baltimore friendship/love affair is a strange one. One that I don't think I will ever understand.

This book was well on its way that week. Mary and I had agreed to commit to this book. It was no longer going to be just a journal. We wanted it to be more. We wanted people to read it. We decided to try to get someone to publish it. We felt that the book had become more than just a few days at the beach, it became something never ending that we wanted to world to read. We believed that we owed it to ourselves to give it a try. It was too powerful to just stay on a computer screen. Our hearts were screaming at us to give this a chance. That brought up one problem. The book was about eighty percent done, and Zack had no clue that it existed.

Mary had not come down to the beach and had left me alone. It was up to me to talk to Zack. I could not tag team with my writer-in-crime to convince him that this was an important thing. I was not sure that I could convince him to let it happen. We were right at that point in the week that we were about to reach the height of our friendship when I decided to talk to him. I thought that that would be the safest course of action. If I did it right away we would still be in the awkward stage, but if I waited too long we would be too tied up in the goodbyes to actually have the conversation. I knew I had to time it perfect.

I pulled Sara over. We swam off from the group for a minute. I needed her for a last minute pep talk. I needed her to reassure me that he could not turn me down. I had done so much work so far that I just couldn't let him put a stop to this book. It was too important to Mary and I. Sara did a fine job of replacing Mary on her first job, which happened to be a major battle. She calmed me down and prepared me to walk over to Zack. I swam up and asked "Can we talk alone real quick?"

We swam a few feet away from the rest of the group so that they couldn't hear what was going on. "So. I have something kind of weird to tell you." I said nervously. "I'm not really sure how to say this, so don't freak out on me if its really weird. Mary and I kind of wrote a book. Its about our story and Mary and Victor's story. We are sending it off to publishing companies, but I need to know that you're okay with it. If you not okay with it I'll change your name or stop it but I just need to know your actual opinion for once."

"Ughh," I knew that it couldn't be good when that sound came out of his mouth. "What do you mean you wrote a book? Well I don't know what to say. I think it is really weird. I don't want to be in a book. What if my friends see it? I just don't really understand this. Why would you want to write a book? I mean I don't know what to do because I don't want to upset Mary because I think it's really important to her."

The piercing words just kept coming out of his mouth. I don't think he realized what he was saying. He just completely was excluding the fact that I had anything to do with the book. I would like to say that was the second worst part of that conversation. He completely denied that I had done anything for this. He denied the years of work that I had done. He kind of denied that I even existed.

Everything got worse, though. He didn't stop there. "I mean I don't even know how you could write a book on that. Nothing happened. I can write our story in one sentence: We took a walk on the beach." I was stunned. Of all of the things that he had said to me over the four year, I think that this was the worst. Did he really just tell me that I meant nothing to him? Did he really just admit that what we had was nothing special? What can you say to that? I stood there in disbelieve wandering if it really ever meant anything to him. It was possible that I was never as important to him as I once thought.

I didn't care that we had been over for four years, and I didn't care that I had a boyfriend that I loved, because it felt like he had just broken up with me right then. I felt the heart break over again. The hardest part of a break up is the realization that they really don't care about you. Then wasn't that kind of what happened? I felt like I had gone nowhere, and he still had every power to hurt me if he pleased. I guess I just always assumed because he was so important to me that I must be important to him too. I guess I was wrong. I guess that I was just some girl who he took a walk with on the beach. I guess everything was just in my head.

I hope that he was just taken off guard. I hate that this part must be shared, but it is important to our story. The two Zacks were back. Whenever, you bring up that first summer, he goes crazy. He just cannot talk about it for some reason. It was a touchy subject for me too, but I didn't go around saying that he was the worst kisser ever. (Which is a lie, it is just an example.) That sealed the deal. Zack was to be nothing to me, nothing more than a friend.

I was still yearning for his approval. He still was not my friend. He still didn't approve of anything that I did. He still didn't approve of me in his life. So I conjured up the perfect payback. I would refuse to let him get rid of me. I was going to force myself into his life, and there was nothing he was going to do about it. I would stay in contact, even when I knew I wasn't wanted. It was not because I need him in my life, but it was because I was annoying him.

The first mission in the payback war was mission "boob bathing suit." Now, I have this one bikini from Wal-Mart. It is a baby blue string bikini that I bought for five dollars the summer before. I don't care that it was cheap and from Wal-Mart, it made my boobs look like a gift straight from God. I walked right up to Zack and said "Zack, I have a serious question to ask you." He agreed to listen to the question, so I proceeded. "How do my boobs look in this bathing suit? Do they look too big?"

He got all flustered and turned away without even looking. "Uh, they look fine."

I had him in my trap! It was the perfect first mission to put him in the most awkward position possible. He didn't know what to do with himself and didn't know how to react. His awkward silence and all around uncomfortableness was broken by Sara and her friend Allison dying in laughter.

After a few months the games subsided and Mary stepped in. She convinced him that the book was a good thing. Well, he is afraid of Mary so I think that had something to do with it. He was all of a sudden on board. He was miraculously okay with whatever I wanted to do and was going to support it. Fear is a wonderful tool.

I chose to believe that Mary was the reason for his change of heart, but maybe I was wrong. Maybe, he realized that he doesn't think before he acts. I think that he is realizing that I have feelings. That sounds bad, so I don't want to say that quite like that. It is more like he is realizing that I exist. I think he is realizing that he cannot run away from me for much longer. I am probably wrong because I cannot speak for him.

Friendship is something that we may never see, but we have achieved tolerance. Zack will always be a part of me. But what will happen next is still left unknown. I cannot lie and say that I wouldn't like to be seen as something in his eyes if it's just friendship, but unlike the past, I will not live my life with a void knowing that I don't have it now. So, to the future, write your ending.

Via Mary
Chapter Twenty-Three: Betrayal

I couldn't tell you how it happened, or even why but before we could try to fix things, they would seem irrevocably broken. You see, Morgan is my best friend, she has been since about 7th grade. Before then we didn't really see eye to eye but that was okay because for whatever reason, Sunset Beach brought us together the year of 7th grade. We did everything together too. It damn near drove our parents insane. Luckily, we only lived ten minutes apart so the commute wasn't too long. Every weekend it was either spent at my house or hers. We didn't have time for anyone else either. Like two peas in a pod, we spent our lives together.

Being that I am a year older than Morgan, actually only 364 days older, yes even our birthdays are a day apart, it made things difficult. We never really fought, besides your typical spats here and there. But we did have maturity issues, as in I would take myself way too seriously and alienate myself from her for a bit, but she was always there to come running back to whenever I needed her. Morgan was like a vital organ to me, without her, I wouldn't exist. You could probably debate that it wasn't healthy, but we didn't care; we were the best of friends, and we would see each other to the end. In fact, I remember going into high school we were worried about losing each other. But here we were at my senior year and her junior year happy as larks that we made it through.

Did I mention that we did everything together? I mean seriously, we took five dance classes together, and we did youth group together as well and that doesn't even factor in our regular hang out time. Everything was going great until that night. We were in my room after youth group one night. All of the sudden, Morgan got really serious.

"Mary can I tell you a secret?" she asked with great concern. "Of course, we're best friends." I answered.

"The truth is, I think I'm anorexic. I've lost thirty pounds in the past two months." She confessed. All I could do is hug her, as she collapsed into my arms. I was so stunned, and shocked, I went blank. Gathering my thoughts I managed to ask her what she wanted to do about all of this. She told me that she wanted help. I freaked out, here stood my best friend who I could have sworn I knew like the back of my hand, yet she had this scary problem that I didn't know how to deal with. We didn't do anything right away. I suggested that we tell my mom and our Aunt Judy (Sara's mom) who is a nurse. She seemed okay with this idea.

That night, I went over our conversation, and I kicked myself for not recognizing the signs. How could I have not noticed that my best friend had lost thirty pounds? That was a lot of weight and I saw her just about every day. This hit me hard, I felt like I had failed her in some way. I needed to get her help, it was the very least I could do. After all this was my best friend, I wasn't going to let her suffer in silence any longer. The more I thought about it the more it made sense, her excuses to skip meals, her labored breathing when she went up flights of stairs, it was all coming together. I kept thinking about it, and as I did I grew more and more scared for her health, and for her life. I mean she lost thirty pound in two months, imagine what she could have lost if I would have let her keep going. I wasn't going to watch my best friend die.

In confidence, I told the three people I trusted the most: my youth minister, and the two directors of our dance school. I knew going into it that it was wrong and there was a chance that Morgan might never talk to me again. It wasn't out of malice, or spite, I was simply worried about my best friend, and wanted to get her help and an answer the best that I could, as fast as I could. I felt like I had to tell them because she was hurting herself and I just wanted it to stop, I wanted her to be better. My youth minister referred me to some great options, but when I told Morgan that I told our youth minister and our dance directors she freaked out thinking that they would tell her parents. I assured Morgan this wasn't the case and that everything would be fine. That's when it got ugly. By telling our youth minister and our dance directors that apparently meant that I told "the world." I felt like I had to tell our dance directors in case she collapsed at dance, which was very likely considering how labored her breathing would get from going up stairs. And dancing was much more laborious than going up a flight of stairs. Looking back, it wasn't my secret to tell and I should have asked before I said anything. But this was my best friend, and I was determined to make her better no matter what it took.

We didn't tell my mom for a few days, and it took even longer for us to tell Aunt Judy. Eventually we told both. They both handled it with such grace and we got Morgan the help she needed. Once we got Morgan the help she needed is when the problems started. She started to seem bitter towards me. Eventually her immediate family stepped in, and that's when it got to it's worst. Ashley is Morgan's older sister, and when she caught wind of what I did, she made it into an all-out war. Morgan and I were now far from friends, but I had no idea that things could actually get worse than they were.

I realized now what I should have seen then; people with eating disorders in general have problems with control, thus the reason for the eating disorder in the first place. By going against Morgan's wishes, I violated her sense of control, thus making it worse for her than getting her better. And oh the price I would have to pay for one set of loose lips even with good intentions.

That summer at the beach it was horrendous to say the least.

First, Sara wasn't staying in our house because Patrick had a baseball tournament so her parents didn't go down at all. So that left me alone and on the defense. At this point, Morgan and I were completely done talking, and to make it worse, her sister Ashley was feeding into my "betrayal" and making Morgan essentially hate me more and more. Unfortunately, Sara was caught in the middle. She wouldn't go against me because she and I were too close for that, but she was staying in the Przybylski house, so she couldn't exactly ignore them either. In any event it was three to one and I wasn't about to challenge it.

Morgan started spreading vicious rumors about my sexuality, and the others were buying into it with no questions asked. For example, Morgan said that I was hooking up with other girls. This was completely false, but when there is a group of kids who are eager to tear you down, they will believe anything. And of course with my luck, Katy Perry's "I Kissed a Girl" was popular that summer, and none of them let me forget the lyrics. Let me tell you, the only thing worse than being called a lesbian when you are, is being called a lesbian when you aren't one because if you ignore the comments, you're inadvertently agreeing with them, and if you deny it you're just adding fuel to the fire. So you're damned if you do and damned if you don't. It got so bad that on Oscar's night I left crying because they were all so hurtful. But I didn't fight back. I refused to get into it, even though the rest of them were closing in on me.

The pain was devastating; I had never felt so alone in my life. I honestly had to look my former best friend in the eye, and what I saw staring back was a complete mystery to me. After all we had been through, I couldn't believe she could turn around and be so hateful. I think the only people more hurt than I was, were my mom and my brother. They wanted so badly to rip the Przybylski family a new one. That was the thing I couldn't get over, there was all of this hate, when in the end, we were all still family. How could we let something so petty destroy our sense of family that easily? It also took a toll on our Pittsburgh friends, they had no idea who to hang out with. But like I said I never fought back, so naturally everyone drifted towards Morgan, Ashley, and Sara.

That vacation honestly felt like the longest week of my entire life. All I did was pray to get through it without crying anymore. After all a family that treats you like that, isn't worth your tears. Although most nights I was left in utter despair, I somehow managed to enjoy myself by reminding myself of the efforts that my PopPop put in to make this house possible. So that year, the vacation was awful but I still held out hope that the next year would be better. Little did I know things were bound to change again?

Via Morgan
Chapter Twenty-Four: "Take Me Away, I Need to Feel the Sand and the Waves."

This book began four years ago. It has been a work in progress. It began as a simple journal. It wasn't a story. It was just a series of events thrown together. I could feel the severity of the situation even in the moment. I knew that it was something that I was going to want to remember as accurately as possible.

Six months rolled around and it was just writing vivid stories. The memories were beginning to fade and I couldn't stand to lose him. I couldn't stand to lose his memory, because that's all I had left.

One day, Mary and I were sitting in my room wallowing in self-pity missing them more than even we could understand. We came up with the crazy idea to write a book. This was three years ago. We didn't think it could be that hard. It was never meant to go anywhere. No one was going to read it but us. Our story had to be written though. We just couldn't let it go. I thought that it would help me forget him. I thought that as soon I was finished it would be over. Or, I thought it could do the opposite. I would finish it, and show it to him, and he would realize he was in love with me again. Either way, it was a win for me.

Zack was my story. He was my life. He was my every thought and memory. Things had to be written. People had to know our story. I believed our message and our story was so powerful that the pages couldn't be left blank. I just needed the world, or at least my world, well, okay, Zack, to realize that I wasn't crazy, but this story was crazy.

Nothing was real until I read it back to myself when it was in print on my computer screen. This story happened. I didn't dream it all up. It made me realize that things like this, things like love, actually happen to real people. It was not something that was just in movies, and it surely was not just for the adults. It was for anyone that had an open enough heart to let it in.

As I read through my own writing to this day, I can't help but remember. I can't help but remember the feeling, the touch, and the smile. Towards the beginning of the story, it made me feel uplifted. It made me realize, maybe love can happen. Maybe love is real, and will find you when you need it the most. I knew that love could conquer all, no matter what the circumstances were.

So how was it that at the beginning of the story, I was joyful and hopeful? I knew how the story would end, considering I lived it but I thought it would change. Why was I expecting for the ending of my own book, or worse my own life, to change? Was this still what I wanted? The more I thought the more confusion spread until my entire body was over come with the terrorizing monster Confucius.

I did not know how to react. I just didn't know what to feel. As I continued to reread the events of my life, everything became real and the hurt came back. I found myself in Mary's car on my way back to school after a serious writing session upset that Zack was no longer in my life. I am not sure if this is just because I wish he was a greater part and wish he was my friend, or if I will always have something special for him deep down in my heart. But how could he still be important to me? It has been years and miles of torment that I would never even dream of venturing back into. Then who is Zack to me today?

As I type, I realize that he is a memory. Well, not just a memory but also a vivid memory or an active memory. He is one person that is impossible to forget in my story, and frankly I never want to forget him. I think back on our story, the ups and the downs, and I realize that I would do it again in a heartbeat. Zack is something that I refuse to regret.

In the past I thought that this book would be my final peace, my final closure. However, everything changed when I believe that it was over. The memories were still there. I could still see his face sitting on the beach building his sand castle on that second day. I just wanted all of this to go away. I just wanted him to go away, so that I could move on with my life. That's when I learned two very important lessons.

The first lesson was you couldn't stop your story. The story of Morgan and Zack will continue for a much longer time and that I am positive of. I am not even sure if there will be a day that he will be completely out of my life. I came to the realization that it was stupid to try to end all ties with him because it was impossible. If I cut off ties with him then I would have to cut off his family, and I could not imagine my life without them. I was just going to have to continue on the road to finding a friendship or at least a tolerance between the two of us. The situation was important to my story. I can't erase him from my life. I see now that if it was not for that half mustached Pittsburghian, I would be lost. Thank you for changing me.

"Memories remain. They persist." Mary Jimenez. That is lesson number two. Those words were spoken in my English 241, Introduction to the Novel, class this first semester of college. The class showed me how important novels were. Stories are important to the author and to even the reader. The whole idea is to touch the reader's heart, and that's what I wanted to do. Okay, going back to the lesson now. After I realized that Zack wasn't the one for me, I began to try to forget him. I never thought that we would be able to be friends again. I thought the only option was to forget what happen or at least pretend that nothing happened. I think I was willing to give up this story to continue to have him in my life. However, just like my professor said "memories persist". I could not escape them how ever hard I tried. As soon as I thought that the memories were leaving me something would remind me of him. For example, I was on my end of senior year trip to Ocean City, Maryland with my friends. We were taking a walk down the beach when I saw it. Right in front of me was a red and white striped umbrella. I frantically looked around the beach looking for him, because he just had to be there! The rest of the week, I had a watchful eye out for him during the day, and at night I tried to drink away his memory.

He will always come back. His memory will always haunt me. The only challenge I now have is how to deal with the constant vexing. Do I celebrate his memory, or do I try to ignore it and push it down into myself every time it "persists?" I think about it often. I think about which course of action would be the best. Every time it arises, I try to find a middle ground, because that's honestly, the only way of dealing with it for now at least. I just hope that one-day Zack and I could be sitting around a sand castle laughing about the past with full confidence that we are good friends. That would be my ideal ending to our story.

Via Mary
Chapter Twenty-Five: Confessions

It is September of my freshman year of college and I found myself in the counseling center at my school. Something really horrible had happened to someone I knew back home and I found it to be hitting me pretty hard, so I decided to go to the counseling office to see if I could talk it out and figure out what was going on. The first session went well, and then I found myself coming back over and over again. There were still some underlying issues that had yet to be resolved.

Before my latest session I decided that instead of going in empty handed, I would bring my handy dandy journal to see if maybe it could give us any clues as to why I was struggling so much. I started paging through it with my counselor and reading aloud entries that I found had the most emotional relevance. It seemed as though that this may be something serious. We decided it would be best if my mom came in and we all three had a chat about the past few weeks of counseling and the possibility of referring me out to a psychiatrist. After many tears and a few confessions later my mom caught on to just how serious this was.

We decided that referring out was the best way to go. I had a psychiatric evaluation and the results were devastating not only for me but for my parents too. The truth is I suffer from Bipolar Disorder as well as Generalized Anxiety Disorder. Both are crippling disorders that prove not only to be taxing on those they afflict but the family of the afflicted as well. At first, I was in shock, I mean I guess I always knew that there was something different about me, but now to have a name to what I considered just an over the top trait was really hard to deal with.

I guess I should explain I'm kind of the golden child in my family. I achieve the grades, I am in the Honors Program at my college, I do extracurricular activities such as: Koinonia, Ad Maiorem, Spring Break Outreach, Connections, Retreats, Rock Climbing, Outdoor Adventure Experience, Evensong, Cristo Rey volunteering and I generally succeed in whatever I delve into. So for me to actually have a problem, in the case two problems, was devastating. Not only that, but I was also a freshman in college, how was I supposed to deal? I began seeing my psychiatrist every three weeks and then as if that weren't enough we started in on the ever-changing slew of medications. Every three weeks they would change, though always emphasizing, "finding the right combination was crucial to my success." Here I am writing this over a year later and we still have yet to find the "right combination." I know I sound bitter, but you would too if your mood changed constantly and when you woke up every morning you had no idea how many times you would cry, or if you could even find the will to get out of bed.

Let me take you on a journey on what it is like to be Bipolar and suffer from anxiety.

Confession: I suffer from Bipolar Disorder and Generalized Anxiety Disorder.

I've never felt more alive or dead.

Confession: Mania controls me in ways no one can really understand.

Mania. I've found that my particular breed of mania comes in two varieties: extreme elation and extreme irritability. Mania is riding a rollercoaster without wearing a seatbelt. Not that it particularly matters to you because safety is the furthest thing from your mind. Your mind, by the way, is going a billion miles per hour. Picture yourself walking along a racetrack, the pace of your walk is the speed at which normal time is progressing, the pace and number of thoughts you are having is equivalent to that of the numerous speeding cars whizzing by you. Oh and as you are walking down the highway don't forget you're in an important conference call about the upcoming event your helping to plan, better pay attention!

Confession: Mania is a social lubricant.

The interesting thing about mania is you don't need drugs or alcohol to get you going, however if offered you'll probably end up taking them anyway because you're the super outrageous fun person that everyone loves. Mania is great. Want to be popular at that school you just transferred to? Sure! With good ol' mania on your side not only do you have a little too much confidence to introduce you to whoever seems appealing at the time, but it makes your brain work extra fast produces those tiny lies that make the person of interest think you are the bee's knees! Your speech is accelerated and your brain reached speeds jets would envy. Because of that fun little connection, while speaking you may slur entire sentences or just completely miss words altogether. And trust me nothing sounds more intelligent the slurred or broken speech!

Confession: I may as well be an insomniac.

I remember one particular episode, it was really late or early depending how you looked at it, probably around 5:00 am and of course I was wide-awake doing a paper for school. Suddenly my mind started really racing and I got so frustrated that I held my head in my hands pleading with my brain to slow down. Spoiler alert: It never slowed down. Then there is the whole situation with sleep. Good luck! It only takes one night of staying up a bit too late for the mania to show you that staying up late is fun, going to bed at 11:00 am and not waking up until 5:30 pm, yeah not so much. So you figure you try to exhaust yourself by not sleeping the whole time and then just going to bed the following night. Of course the adrenaline runs out and that thirty-minute power nap becomes a five-hour snooze. So much for the day! The mania-sleeping schedule is particularly a blast when you live with parents who get up and go to work around 5:00 am. Sure you can feign sleep, but what's the point? Chances are they heard you clonking around all night anyway. Their advice is the obvious: call the doctor and set up an appointment. Too bad you sleep through the office hours rendering it literally impossible to get back into scheduled visits. Oh and the one time that you can go is for the Saturday hours, which is the only day the secretary isn't in so you have no hope of scheduling a follow up appointment and before you know it your out of meds and back into the super delightful and always exciting world that is mania. Speaking of medication, did you know that behind people with schizophrenia, people with bipolar disorder have the highest rate of non-compliance?

Confession: Concentration is a joke.

The other great thing about mania, if all its perks haven't already seduced you, is it won't let you concentrate on anything. You get hit with sensory overload and you can kiss your assignment, no matter how important it may be, goodbye. Mania doesn't care if your paper is worth 20% of your grade, it has it's own agenda. An agenda that had you been medicated, you would have ran away from as fast as possible. Mania is the equivalent of watching a movie on fast-forward in your head. You have all of these blurry images running through your head but they go so fast that you don't have any time to make sense of them, let alone think about anything else. Mania makes you try things you would have never previously consider: drugs, piercings, partying, and skydiving are the most memorable. Remember that extreme and irrational fear of heights that you have? Well all you need is a little manic episode to make you jump out of that plane and free fall 9,000 feet and parachute down another 5,000. Sounds fun until on one of your even days you almost have a panic attack because of the realization of what you put yourself through

Confession: Mania is and very well could be the end of most of my friendships.

But that is only the elated side of mania; there is still the mania that severs ties, also known as extreme irritability. Everything is going great in mania-land, until that one little thing happens, it can be as subtle as a reminder from your mom to call the doctor to schedule an appointment, to your roommate talking a little to loud on the phone while you're trying to do homework. The barrier goes up and suddenly every little thing that anyone does is the most annoying thing that they could possibly do. Yes, asking you how your day was is so annoying that all you can do is answer using the fewest amount of words possible or else you might explode. Why do they want to know about your day anyway? It was the same as any other damn day, who cares? What was that? Your mom moved your car keys from the dining room table to your dresser? What the hell was she thinking? Those are YOUR keys, how dare she move them from where you left them? And though to the sober mind it seems petty, you are so ready to rip your mother a new one that your blood teems with anger.

And forget joking around, absolutely not! Your dad playfully makes a remark at the fact that you were using his chair in the computer room? Well the rational reaction is of course to slam your laptop shut, and march up the stairs promptly ignoring the hurt and confusion on his face when he sees he stepped over a line that he didn't realize was there. That's the thing with the extremity of irritability it draws lines everywhere that it is so impossible to navigate a normal life. How can you when you are so busy tearing apart everyone around you, not because it makes you feel better but because people seem so utterly unaware of all of their tragic flaws. Extreme irritability makes you super fun to be around. Especially when it cuts off your communication skills because you are so hypercritical about the person you are attempting to talk to. While they are trying to carry on a normal conversation you are mentally begging them to shut up and go away because the only remedy for irritability is complete solitude, which by the way you'll never get with your brother listening to the TV in the other room at a volume that even the deaf could hear.

Confession: Mania and Anxiety may as well be a deadly cocktail.

Mania makes you hyper aware of your surroundings which in turn, at least for me, creates a little treasure I like to call, anxiety. Do you have any idea what its like to wake up and the first thing you notice is; it's quiet, so you then check out the window and sure enough all of the cars are gone, which means of course everyone is at work. Following this train of thought it means your dear sweet mother drove to her job as a preschool teacher all by herself, and although it's a nice fifteen minute drive, there are deer on the road so early in the morning, maybe she reached down to adjust the radio and while she wasn't looking one jumped out in front of the car and now she's really hurt. Filled with fear and anxiety you grab the phone and call her and when she calmly answers the phone despite the screaming five year olds in the background your mind is put at ease. Temporarily. Until you realize she still has the whole ride home to accidently kill herself. And of course on some days, though you know she should be due home around 1:30 pm or 2:00 pm you quickly realize it's 3:00 pm. Instead of calling her like a normal human being you proceed to pace around the house, presuming her to be dead, until her car pulls up in the driveway with bags of groceries, from her obvious trip to the store, that she in haste, neglected to tell you she was making that afternoon.

Confession: At least with Depression I'm not hurting

myself.

Depression. As awful as this may sound, I quite fancied the depression more than the mania. You can sleep through depression, and though you may find yourself to be a bit sluggish, it's at least bearable. Depression however dulls everything down, except of course emotions. Emotions are always heightened. There have been times where I find myself burrowed under my blankets crying in agony because I feel so utterly helpless. And the tears? I've cried so hard and for such extended periods of time, I'm talking three to six hours just non-stop crying, for absolutely no reason. My poor friends, they would sit there and try to consol me for the first hour or two but even they have breaking points. It's been so bad that they have had to take shifts. Not that they had ever thought I'd hurt myself, I've always had enough sense to never to do that. However I can't tell you how much pain I've caused them by being in such a constant state of agonizing grief. It can ware a person down. Depression is a vast nothingness. The best way I can describe my darkest moments, is the feeling of being chained to nowhere. Most of the time there isn't even a real problem. There is just nothing, and a lot of it at that. Nothing accompanied by the agony of the realization that there is nothing. And lets be honest, how easy do you think it is to explain, nothing. There were days when I couldn't bare to get out of bed. Not because I didn't want to, I just couldn't summon the will to produce movement, except of course from my tear ducts. Depression is like running a marathon except you're running in slow motion, while everyone else is passing you by with great ease. You expend great effort too, to try and get to the end, but you can't no matter how hard you try, the hollowness of your existence, which should make you feel weightless, instead makes you feel heavy.

Confession: I never knew how devastating nothing was.

Depression makes you do nothing. You eat nothing, you feel

nothing, you want nothing, and words are scarce because to gather the strength to make sentences is always too great a feat. Speaking as someone who tends to be rather meticulous about person hygiene, depression even takes that away from you. You lose sight of the reason to shower, to get out of bed, and to carry on with life. Not that ending it is the solution; the solution more often then not is to just do nothing. To let life go and live in nothingness. Sometimes the most powerful emotion is a blunt dullness. You lose everything to depression too. You draw the shade, because even the light of day is too much to handle. Not that you could see it from underneath the copious amounts of blankets you piled on yourself. When it gets really bad, you even start to lose friends. But you can't really blame them, would you want to be around someone who did nothing all the time? I think not! The pain that should be there from the loss of the friendship surprisingly isn't there at all, because at this point you're numb. You're incapable of feeling anything, which in turn leads you to feel nothing. The cozy shell of nothingness practically swallows you whole.

Depression is frustrating. Being that I consider myself someone who is rather expressive and creative, I always want to go to bed knowing that I did my best in all of the days activities. However when depression strikes there is nothing you can do but wait it out and hope that it won't last for long. Granted these are all hopes in hindsight because during the episode you are so engrossed in emotion that rational thought escapes you.

The other frustrating aspect is that I consider myself to be someone who is pretty good at knowing when to ask for help. Even depression takes that away from you. Depression is also frustrating in that it makes you believe that no one could ever understand what you are going through, when in truth if you were actually physically able to talk, someone probably could help you through it. It's like trying to take a nice jog outside in the winter at first you realize its cold outside but then before you know it you're running in the driving snow and there is nothing you can do about it and you're stuck until it clears. No matter how badly you want to get out you can't and of course no one else can you see you because you're M.I.A. from life. Depression is also frustrating because when you start something, say a club, you suddenly lose interest and have no desire but to stop going, and you do. It's like grasping your hopes and dreams and then haphazardly letting them go because you just don't feel like holding on to them anymore. And once you let go the damage is done and there is nothing you can do because more often than not depression leaves you in the rubble of its most recent disaster and it's nearly impossible to dig yourself out of such a deep hole.

Confession: Depression is like a leech

It slowly drains you of life until you are quite literally paralyzed by nothingness. In a way I suppose I am lucky that my bipolar disorder creates more mania because at least it makes me function, even if its usually over the top. Depressive episodes can also lead to different thoughts, now I've never experienced suicidal thoughts, but I have experienced those of harming myself, never fatally however. My go-to thought whenever I am in a depressive episode is always about getting in a car crash. I always entertain the idea of what it would be like to get into a car crash that would put me in a coma for a few days and then I would wake up and make a full recovery, but those days spent in the hospital, always seemed so appealing when I was in a depressive state. I don't know if it was attention that I craved or if I just needed to sink back into the nothingness that depression would so often consume me in. The depressive episodes also made me have violent thoughts but again it was never anything that would cause a fatality. I don't know why that is. I suppose underneath all of the emotion and the turmoil that is caused by bipolar disorder, I have a strong will to live and to survive. I can honestly say that I love my life, and I feel blessed to have the family and friends that I do.

I would never want to do something as selfish as hurt my well being because I wouldn't ever want those around me to suffer through that.

So that is what it is like to be bipolar and anxious. Luckily now I am back on medication and I am seeing a counselor once a week to get myself back together and healthy. I think one of the most amazing things about going through all of this is the support I've received from those around me. For example, Victor: when I told him about it his response wasn't one of disgust or ignorance. Instead he told me that he would always be there for me. He told me that he wished I had told him sooner so he could be there through it with me. I can't explain just how amazing he is. His unconditional support and love have made this road to recovery so much easier and uplifting.

Via Mary
Chapter Twenty-Six: Magis

I wouldn't feel right about writing this book unless it contained this chapter. I want to take the time to talk about the man behind the beach house, also known as my PopPop. I only had him in my life for eleven years, but now that I'm going on twenty, I have realized more than ever before the importance of remembering him.

"Magis," a Latin word meaning, "the more" or "the greater" which I believe is the way that my grandfather lived his life. He was always doing things for a greater purpose, and his life was never really about him. Though he may not have realized it at the time, through the way he lived his life, he set an example of what it was to live for magis. He served in the Marines, worked for the government, and even opened up his own baseball memorabilia shop. He did all of this to provide for his wife, Adelina (or as I refer to her, MomMom) and his two sons my dad, Joe, and my Uncle Richard. He also coached baseball and football on the side for fun. As for the Marines their motto is Semper Fidelis or always faithful, a phrase that my grandfather lived out every day of his life.

His heart was one that was filled with so much love that when my brother, my cousins, and I came around he was practically overflowing with it. That's how we got the beach house in the first place. You see, my grandfather had a huge obsession with golf, and South Carolina being the golf capital of the USA (I only know this because golf is like a religion to my family, or so it seems) it seemed like the perfect place to go at first. Then Erik, myself, and

Sara were born and he decided to buy a property (on a golf course, go figure!) so his grandchildren would always have a place to go to vacation. I know most grandparents are big on buying presents but really? A house? The man was crazy, but so well intentioned that it all came out as love.

Like I said, my PopPop loved golf, and he was always eager to share himself with us, his grandchildren, so what did he do? He made his backyard into a mini golf course. I'm talking holes and flags with the little numbers on them and everything! And when Erik got the first hole in one my grandfather actually went through the trouble of having a plaque made up for him saying something like "#1 Golfer." His excessive love and kindness set the mold for what my cousins and I are like today. Not that we are landscapers and build golf courses or anything but hey, in my grandfather's eyes we could do anything!

Just like many grandparents around the world my PopPop was a huge gift giver, the man practically made every excuse in the book to give you a gift. Oh it's Wednesday? Here have a present! His favorite thing to do when he went down to the beach house in SC would be to bring his grandchildren back gifts. Now I have reason to believe that I was his favorite grandchild because every time he would give us presents from the beach he would always sneak me in his bedroom and give me an extra present. Now that I'm older, I'm pretty sure he did this with all four of us but I like to think it was just me. The man loved to shop so much so that he went all the way down to North Carolina to get Patrick a Tickle Me Elmo for Christmas because they were sold out in Maryland.

One of my favorite memories of my grandfather is the one and only day that he picked me up from middle school. We were making conversation in the car and he asked me what I had done the prior weekend. I told him about how I went to the Reese Carnival with my friend Lauren and got funnel cake. I told him just how much I loved funnel cake, which, back in my pudgy adolescent days was a lot! That Christmas we proceeded to go up to MomMom and PopPop's to celebrate as usual. The first thing we did was open gifts, and I had gotten through all of mine in a rush because when you are ten years old that's all you do! Then my PopPop told me to hold on, and he went back into his infamous bedroom and came out with a pretty big box. Low and behold I rip it open and there sitting before me is a funnel cake maker. All because I had mentioned it in passing in one conversation! It was only after his passing that I would come to find out that he travelled all the way down to Virginia to buy it for me because he couldn't find one in the tri-state area. Again, all because I had mentioned it in one little conversation! If that doesn't display excessive love and kindness than clearly I need a refresher on what exactly those are.

There was really only one problem, how was I ever going to find a man to match up to the man that my grandfather was? My grandfather was a man of integrity, one who lived his truths as authentically as possible. I couldn't fathom replacing him let alone trying to find someone who even matched his caliber. The only person I knew who could even step up to the plate lived over a thousand miles away, and I hadn't seen him in years. This was a doozy if I've ever seen one before!

Via Mary
Chapter Twenty-Seven: The Visit

It has been three years since I last saw his face. Three years since he held me in his arms. Three years since I looked into the magnificently crystal blue eyes. But all of this was about to change because in exactly one hour and ten minutes I was going to see him. It should have just been ten minutes, but his flight got delayed, which left Sara, Morgan, and me stuck in the airport for an hour and ten minutes. Morgan also had the opening shift at her work, which required her to be up at 4:30 am, or something ridiculous like that. His flight was due in at 10:00pm but it would be 11:00pm before he actually got to us.

My nerves were going crazy; I couldn't believe that I was actually going to see the man I loved for the first time in three whole years. The funny thing was Sara, Morgan and I thought we were in the right part of the airport but when it came time to get him we soon realized that we were in the wrong part of the airport. How stupid could we be? This was BWI we've been here a bunch of times. So that resulted in us sprinting across the airport, in heels mind you, to get to the right part before he came out and realized just how incompetent we were. When we finally got to the right part of the airport the passengers weren't even out yet so we were all relieved, except for me. I was incredibly nervous, I hadn't seen Victor in three years now, what if he didn't like what he saw? After all I was skinnier back then, my hair was longer and blonder back then as well. What if he thought I was ugly? What if my personality wasn't the same in person? Of course I knew he loved me, but still, guys are much more stimulated by looks than girls are, what if I wasn't good enough anymore?

Looking back to the terminal gates, passengers were starting to get off the plane. My nerves increased infinitely. This was it. I put my sign down, (yes we made signs), and I waited to see my love. Morgan was on camera duty; she was going to take the reuniting picture of us. He must have sat in the very back of the plane because it seemed like everyone and their mother had already gotten off the plane yet no Victor. Then I saw this really tall guy, he was wearing a black shirt, the rest didn't matter, it was him. It was my Victor. I ran into his arms, he smiled, I didn't let go. He was everything in that moment; it could have lasted forever for all I cared.

After I finally let go, he went over and greeted the other two girls, who I forgot were even there, he was all I needed. We finally got to the car after we scurried around the airport. He made fun of us for having no idea where we were in our home airport, but that was okay because at least now we were all together and that was truly all that mattered. Now finding the car was a tricky business and the ride home was even worse. In order to get home we were supposed to take the beltway except for the fact that the exit to get on 695 was completely blocked off. So panic set in. With music blasting, Sara talking, Victor in the front seat talking, and Morgan frantically on the phone with her mom, I had about had it.

"Shut up!" I screamed as I turned the music off. "I'm lost, it's dark, it's late, and I need to get everyone home in one piece so everyone please shut up!" I said, regaining my nerve. After that mini breakdown Morgan got directions and we were home free.

Back at my house Morgan and Sara said their goodbyes. Victor and I headed inside, and went straight downstairs, it was past midnight and I didn't want to wake up my parents. We got settled and then it occurred to me. What were we going to do? I didn't have much in the house and certainly didn't even think to plan for downtime. So we just started to talk. And then for the first time he held me in his arms. I couldn't help but think that this was perfect. The big question on my mind was, would we kiss, if so, when? After all, with my type "A" personality these things had to be planned! So there we were lying down on the air mattress just making light conversation and in the middle of my sentence, he popped his head up and kissed me. Just like that. It was that simple. I couldn't help but be thrilled. The kissing continued here and there. But my favorite thing would have to be when I was laying next to him and he would swoop me up into his arms. For once, I felt at peace, just like I did in the ocean with him four years ago. I didn't need some sloppy grand display of affection; I just needed him. It was so exciting to go to bed at night and wake up the next day knowing he would be under the same roof as me.

Over his time spent in Maryland we went to the National Aquarium, The Baltimore Zoo, and Hershey Park. The weekend reaffirmed all of our feelings for each other. We had a nice long talk in the car ride home from Hershey Park. We talked again about marriage, what we wanted, religion and everything we talked about during those five days at the beach. I was more in love with him than I ever had been before. I couldn't believe he was real and he was in my car with me and we were finally together. I felt so blessed to even know him.

We were two of a kind and everyone that I introduced him to thought the same too. The most important thing that we did that weekend was I introduced him to my grandmother whom I refer to as Nannie. My Nannie is by far one of the most important people in my life. I'm exactly like her too. Well maybe a little less worrisome but for the most part, my Nannie and I are two birds of a feather. Meeting her was a big step because before him I had only ever introduced her to one other of my significant others. Luckily for me he passed with flying colors. Every time I see her now she always asks about him and wonders how he is doing. This means so much to me more than either of them will ever understand. My mom and dad were also huge fans of his. And I couldn't be more thrilled about it.

I think my favorite moment happened the night before he left. We were sitting in the living room just chatting. I was talking about my favorite TV show and how it was coming on in an hour. It's kind of a girly show and I wasn't sure if he would be interested in watching it with me. So naturally I asked if it was okay, if not I could always record it and watch it later. And then he said the words that for whatever reason had a huge effect on me, he said, "Mary, if you want to watch it, then we will watch it."

In that moment I couldn't help but think of the story my Nannie told my about my Granddad (her husband.) It was Christmas and they were working on the Christmas tree, and my dad was coming to pick up my mom to take on a date. My Nannie kept making my Granddad move the tree from place to place around the room, of course ending up in the first place that they put it.

My dad then said to my Granddad, "Roland, why do you put up with that?"

And my Granddad responded, "Joe, it's Christmas, just do what they ask."

I guess my point is, in that moment, my Granddad's adoration and love for my Nannie was so obvious and simple and Victor saying something of similar caliber really touched me even though he had no idea that he did that. It was just one of the many moments that remind me how much he loves me even if he doesn't know he's doing it.

The marvel with him continued because while we were out on the town doing the different activities I had planned for us he was a perfect gentleman. He held my hand, hugged and kissed me just when it was appropriate. It was truly a remarkable time. I think the quote of the trip was, "Man you sure like to hold hands a lot." I wanted the trip to last forever. It was the perfect amount of time though, just enough to reconnect but not too long where I would get super attached and then have huge breakdown afterward. In fact I must say I didn't even cry when he left! Though I was working so I didn't get to take him to the airport, so my mom did and apparently he really impressed her on their drive over there. This made me incredibly happy. I couldn't have asked for a more blessed long weekend.

Via Mary
Chapter Twenty-Eight: Discovery

The visit had left me in awe of Victor. I couldn't believe how well it went. But seeing Victor wasn't the only thing it was good for. Victor coming had forced Morgan and I to break our painful silence. It wasn't immediate, but eventually the walls came down, and we were back to being the old pals that we had once been.

The one thing that I never clearly understood was why we stopped being friends in the first place. I knew that there was tension over the way her eating disorder had been disclosed, but I wasn't stupid. I knew that there had to be more to the story than that. So, a few weeks before Victor was due to fly out, I invited Morgan out to our favorite restaurant, California Pizza Kitchen, to sit down and talk. To my surprise, she agreed to come. Maybe she was willing to surrender too? I was painfully nervous on the drive over to Hunt Valley. I couldn't believe that we had become so estranged, and the more I thought about the whole situation, the more I realized that she was a complete stranger to me. I got there first, of course. That just made it worse, because it gave me time to think. And as I hope you have come to realize, thinking and me don't go together very well.

When she finally got there, we were seated and got to talking. It wasn't as awkward as I thought it was going to be. We mainly reminisced over past times that we had been here together. We flirted around the real issues that we both knew we came to talk about. Neither of us was brave enough to bring it up though. So, I finally held up my white flag, and asked the question that both of us were avoiding.

"So Morgan, what exactly happened to us?" I asked softly, as if I didn't want her to hear what I was saying.

She smiled as she responded with a simple, "I don't know."

Great, we were really going to flit around the issues all night. I don't know if she was being genuine or if she just wasn't ready to talk about it. I gave her the benefit of the doubt and decided she just wasn't ready to talk about it. So I decided to man up and admit defeat.

"Look Morgan, I honestly don't know what happened between us. So I just want to say that I am so sorry for whatever I did to you that made you stop talking to me. I can't tell you how incredibly horrible I felt about this whole situation." I apologized profusely, but she seemed unmoved. She didn't really say anything about it, aside from acknowledging that I said what had I said. Still she didn't provide any explanation as to why things happened the way they did. I grew frustrated at our lack of progress. I am one of those forgive and forget type of people so the fact that it wasn't happening that way messed with my patience. That night we left dinner with an amount of progress that seemed as if we didn't even go to dinner at all.

Victor's visit came around, and I invited Morgan to come with me to the airport to pick him up. She surprised me again when she agreed to come, even though she had to work early the next morning. Morgan, Sara, and I all bantered lightly, in the car ride there as if we were actually all friends. When in truth, Sara and I were friends, and Morgan and Sara were friends, but Morgan and I were still a huge question mark. Nonetheless she came to the airport with me. That was the only time that she saw Victor. I invited her and her boyfriend Pablo, to come with us to different places but Morgan always politely declined.

After Victor's visit is when things got interesting. I had made many awkward attempts at talking to Morgan, when I finally found a common thread that actually got us to talk. Our "book" project that we had always jokingly talked about was the common thread. You see, we always joked about turning our journal entries and stories into a book about the boys and our experiences with them. But now it seemed as if we actually had enough material to actually make it into a book. So I egged her on about actually committing to it. Surprising me yet again, she agreed.

The book consumed us, and it also forced us to talk again and share memories. Eventually we also confronted our issues, and got past them. Finally, we could start into the new territory of a friendship. This was a wary situation for both us because neither of us knew if we could trust the other. Slowly we opened up and as we were forced to spend more time together. The only real problem that I had was Ashley. She was yet again being over protective of Morgan. I knew that if this kept continuing Morgan and I would never have a real shot of being friends. I needed both of them to see that I wasn't the enemy, and furthermore, I never was the enemy. The way we all came together was actually really random. It involved two phone calls that I was forced to make because of a phone call my mother got. I know this all sounds weird and vague so allow me to explain.

During my sophomore year of college, I had to take off the first semester due to my on-going battle with Bipolar Disorder and Generalized Anxiety Disorder. Most of my family wasn't even aware that I had these problems because I decided that I would have people find out on a need to know basis. Besides, I really don't like attention, and I knew this would stir up a lot of it if I made a big show out of it. Anyways, one night my Aunt Claire, Ashley and Morgan's grandmother called the house looking for my dad but instead my mom answered the phone. Earlier in the week she had stopped by to drop off a book for him and I had accidentally let it slip that I was taking the semester off but I didn't say why. While on the phone with my mom, my Aunt Claire must have brought it up to inquire as to why I wasn't in school. My mom started off vague, but I just told her to tell her the truth. The problem there is once Aunt Claire knows something, the whole world knows it. I knew I didn't want Ashley and Morgan to find out about it this way; I wanted to be the one to tell them.

So I quickly grabbed my phone and called Ashley first, and got her voicemail, I left one instructing her to call me back, I proceeded to call Morgan and got her voicemail as well. Ashley called back first and I explained the whole story to her; to my surprise she was rather receptive to it. Then I said what I really wanted and needed to say.

"Ash, I know that we have a history of not getting along very well but I just want to say that we are family and we should be there for each other. I want to apologize for the way things went with Morgan and everything that followed the incident." I gushed. She surprised me again when she agreed with me that we needed to stick together. It was a really emotional phone call to say the least. Finally, I had Ashley on my side, and maybe just maybe we could become friends too. Morgan eventually called me back to and I basically reiterated what I said to Ashley, to Morgan. She was just as receptive as Ashley was, and I think it aided in breaking down some of the walls, now that they both saw that I was just as vulnerable as they were.

So my friendship with Morgan rose from the ashes and day-by-day became stronger. We eventually started hanging out, outside of working on the book. It was nice to have her back in my life. I wasn't sure what to call her though, was she my cousin? My friend? My best friend? The politics were really confusing about the whole thing. Now that everything was straightened out with Morgan, I felt free enough to finish the book with confidence that we would have a friendship outside of our work. It was a long road to get to where we are today, but luckily the dark period between us was over. And it was just that, a period of time, something fixed, and now, I knew it would soon be a distant memory.

Via Mary
Chapter Twenty-Nine:
Calm Before the Storm

I want to take the time to remember my PopPop because if it weren't for him I would have never met Victor in the first place. If it weren't for his excessive love and kindness, who knows where we would be. So for the gift of that house, and for all of the love and support he gave me while he was alive, I owe him much thanks. I can only hope to learn to love as deeply and excessively as him. While he was here he held an infinite amount of kindness in his heart and he captivated many people around him. He saw to it that Erik, Sara, Patrick, and I never went without by any means, and for that I am forever grateful.

I can't think of a better person to be in love with. I mean, who after a petty disagreement would stay up all night just to wish me good morning and tell me they love me? Victor is truly an amazing man who has outstanding character. He considers himself lucky to have me, but in truth, I'm the lucky one. I cannot imagine my life without him, and I hope that he feels the same way about me. With my fingers crossed, I think it's safe to say that our love is real and will last beyond a lifetime. Every day I am not with him I miss him.

It is now about three weeks since Victor has visited, and my heart aches in his absence. I haven't spoken to him in three days, not because we are fighting or anything, but he is currently in basic training for the Air Force. Basic training of course means that there is a moratorium on communication with the exception of writing letters. Victor, however, being the headstrong person that he is decided that we shouldn't exchange addresses because he wants to be completely independent for once. Though I disagree with this idea, and it really hurts me, I know that it's for the best. Besides, it's only two months, and we've gone without talking for longer before. More important, if not most importantly, I love him and I'm okay with making this sacrifice for him because of that.

To me, loving someone isn't about what's best for you. It's about caring so deeply for another's well being that you are willing sacrifice your own self-interest, in the betterment of the other person. So although I am saddened at the notion of not talking to him for at least two months, I know that I am doing my best to do what his right for him. Don't get me wrong, I already miss the sound of his voice, and I cried on Skype the last time we talked. Oh and did I mention, I also made him leave me a voice-mail so I would have something to listen in the months that I wouldn't be able to talk to him? Yeah, that happened. So I am not apathetic to the situation in any way, I just want to do the right thing, even if it's the hard thing.

After all this is just another way of testing our relationship, as if the 15 hours of distance, sparse time together, other people, and fighting weren't enough. But I have to remember what my grandfather said, "Improvise, Adapt, and Overcome." This I feel is the only way to get through this, and the only way to get through life. So far we've conquered the distance, sparse amount of time together, and the other people simply by taking time to talk more, figure out why we fell in love in the first place. Now I won't say we don't fight because everyone fights and it would be a lie to try and pretend that we didn't. However we are the lucky ones because the fights are stupid and short, and in the end love conquers our fighting. Our love is simple; it's for the most part easy although the situation we're in is difficult. But that's the thing about life, it's not always going to be easy, and no one ever said it was. Sure there are easier moments sometimes, but for the most part it's challenging, and it's how you face those challenges that brings out your true character. So I'll wait for him with the piece of mind that he misses me just as much as I miss him, and that when the time is right for him, I'll hear from him again. Though it may not be as soon as I would prefer, it isn't about me it's about him.

I don't think I could ever explain the depth of our love. It's something hard for even myself to fathom. But I know one thing and that is that this is the most real emotion I have ever dared to feel. He is the one person I know I will love all of my life. After all, that's why I wrote this story. Our love is pure and its beautiful and it's everything my five-year-old daydreams could have ever asked for. He has become such a big part of my life and it's hard to think that I could have ever existed without him. It only took five days to irrevocably give my heart away. A decision most logically sound people would disagree with. But loves knows no logic, and apparently, neither do I. So I will continue to love him to incomprehensible depths and know in my heart of hearts that he feels the same way.

Now that Victor has visited, things of course have changed. I can't describe the feeling of being around him. I sit here writing this, four years later to the exact day, still just as, if not more in love with him than I was before. He's all I want and all I need. I hold great hope for the future but for now I am completing college and Victor is starting Basic Training for the Air Force. We both have big plans, and we're the type of people that will accomplish them. You see, that's what attracted me to him in the first place. I've always viewed him as driven, and determined. I saw it in our friendly wave riding competition, and although I can't witness basic training, his reasons behind going into the service are proof enough for me. All I can say is I am proud of him, and I'm proud to know him. I couldn't ask for a better person to love and be loved by. So I guess we were never supposed to work out. We were fifteen and had over 1000 miles of distance between us; this should have just been a summer romance. But luckily, for us, we were the exception to the rule. We were the special two and there is no one I would rather be with even though I am only with him for a maximum of a week or two per year.

Via Mary
Chapter Thirty: Shattered

Fast-forward three months, and things have taken a turn for the worst. Victor is in Tech School for the Air Force, and we seldom talk. I know that he has important things to do, so I don't really expect to hear from him. When I do it's always a blessing. I cherish every moment that we get to talk. But sooner than I would come to realize, it would be the end. This chapter would close, and I would be forced to open a new chapter that I never even realized could be.

It started with one ill-fated phone conversation. Before I could stop myself, I hung up the phone on him. This may have been the last time that we ever spoke. Victor said the words that I didn't even know existed, "I don't love you anymore." And just like that, the fairytale was over. I shouldn't have been surprised. I should have seen this coming. The shortened phone calls, the forced "I love you's", and the nothing fights. All of the signs were there but I was so blinded by the hope of it working out that I failed to see it. My heart dropped into my stomach, this couldn't really be happening.

It took me awhile to cry. But just as soon as I was wondering why I wasn't crying, I was in my mother's arms, sobbing. I was so inconsolable that my mother had no idea what to do with me. Instead of asking questions, she just stayed there with me as I continued to sob and wail. My heart ached at the realization that this was really over. My body physically hurt to move, I wasn't interested in neither food nor drink. It felt like my soul was twisting and turning and being ripped to shreds as I spiraled out of control. I couldn't regain control over my body, the tears just kept coming every time I thought I had composed myself, I would just start crying more. I laid in bed for days, and did nothing. I shut everyone out. I wasn't interested in the rest of the world; I was only interested in this gaping wound in my chest, where my heart used to beat. The more I cried the more hollow I felt. It seemed as if my existence was shrinking, and soon there would be nothing left.

With my head in my hands, I tried to collect myself but I couldn't. I couldn't stop the tears. My eyes grew red and sore. I wailed, and I half screamed into my pillow. I couldn't help it, the anguish overtook me as I realized that I was finally alone. I was devastated. Inconsolable doesn't even begin to describe how I felt. The gut wrenching sobs continued as I thought about the past four years. What the hell was I supposed to do without him? This wasn't a part of the plan. What happened to happily ever after? I screamed and I cried and was completely overtaken by the utter sorrow. Each tear went right down to the core of me. I was weak and I was scared in realizing that there was a whole world out there that I finally had to face, alone.

The truth is, I am just a disillusioned teenager who put all of her hope into something that is bigger than herself, hoping to gather some kind of meaning out of it. Okay maybe that is just a touch too bitter. If I were to describe myself at all it would be awestruck. I never imagined that this would end. Everything seemed to be going okay. Though we didn't get to talk often, and though most of the time it was quick, it seemed like enough to get us by. I was so comfortable in "us." How could we possibly end? But as my PopPop would say, "The facts are the facts. You can't ignore them." And the fact that he no longer loved me was definitely something that I couldn't get around. I was forced to let this part of my life go. Call me dramatic but I was uncertain of how I would go on with life without him there. I wasn't going to be stupid about it and rush into being friends again. I needed time to heal, you see, I always try to make hard times into growing points. Though it is never easy, it's doable, and that is what I had to hold onto.

This was going to be the most painful thing that I could ever do. As I sit here, locket in hand, I take it off from around my neck. I study it. I stare at the pretty design and debate on opening it and looking at the four seashells. The seashells that have come to be so much more than random pieces of the ocean that I stole off of the beach that summer. I open it and delve into an easier time, a time when hearts weren't strewn across the floor, and love was abundant. Snapping back to reality I realize that, that time is over. I realize that I may never see or hear from Victor again. I toy with this idea, and as I do tears begin to form behind my eyes. I don't cry, not yet. Instead I drift back to that seemingly endless summer. The memories flash before my eyes like a movie, a tear slides down my cheek. I feel empty at the realization that I all I have now are memories. Victor will just be a memory. With every beat of my heart I feel an intense pang of sorrow.

No longer would I be able to hear his voice tell me that he loves me. In that moment I realize that I may never want to hear those words ever again. The thought of there ever being someone else sickens me. The idea of never being wrapped up in his arms comes to mind. Internally, I beg myself not to cry, not to let myself get this wrapped up in the pain and to just let it go. The gut wrenching sobs begin. How could he discard me from his life so easily? Did I really make it that easy for him to just up, and leave? I know I will eventually exhaust myself into a peaceful sleep. But the consolation ends there because every dream becomes a nightmare; it's always about him. Upon waking I check my phone to see if he has come to his senses and decided to take me back, he never does. Soon my life becomes a waking nightmare. I beg every phone call, text, facebook notification, and email to be him.

It never is. This is rock bottom.

Weeks pass, at this point even my friends are getting impatient with my grieving process. The only one who understands is Morgan, because of Zack, of course. It's frustrating because I know that many people, especially all of my friends have never felt what I had for four and half years with Victor. It's frustrating to know that they will never understand the depth of love that I experienced. And it's even more frustrating to know that they will never be able to understand because I can't even properly express it. I'd even boast that most married couples would never experience the deep, unconditional, and breath-taking love that I experienced with Victor, no matter how long they are married. So of course I will grieve, over the gaping hole in my chest. And I will cry, scream, and wail over the loss of the only real thing I've ever felt. Though I know I need to pick up the pieces and trudge forward, I can't see myself enjoying the journey.

I ponder the idea of moving on. I ponder the idea of a life without Victor. I lose myself in thought, as more memories chase away my sanity. My mind drifts in and out of thought. And after all the thinking I had done there was really only one question left, where do I go from here?

Via Mary
Chapter Thirty-One: Higher Ground

Usually, if not always, I have a plan. I know exactly what to do and how things will turn out because I stress over carefully calculating each outcome. For this, I had no response. No plan. No nothing. So what was I going to do? Baby steps. For a while I didn't smile, I couldn't. The gesture seemed too painful, and too fake. I wasn't okay. I struggled. So many times I picked up my phone, scrolled through my contacts, found his name, and just as I was about to press send, something came over me. What was the big deal? I mean he was just a boy, yes a boy not a man, I mean we were both kids! Though I seemingly loved beyond what most would consider logical, what did it matter because just like that, I lost it. But so what? I could love again if I tried really hard. So why not? I wasn't chained to him anymore. It was time to let him go.

But it wasn't that easy, I couldn't just let him go. He simply meant too much to be tossed aside on a whim. After all this was four years of my life that I wasn't going to get back so I decided a little self pity wouldn't hurt anybody. Instead, I decided to take it slow. Figure out who I was without him. To be honest, there wasn't much to start with; I didn't realize how co-dependent I had become. I decided it was best to sift through all of the memories first, you know, get it all out before having to finally let go. I looked through all of our photos together, and I reread journal entries that I wrote about our time together. I can't lie and say that it was easy, and that I didn't cry repeatedly. But this was going to be okay, at least that's what I told myself. I fought every day to be okay. I wasn't even going for happy, just okay would be enough for me.

Like a caterpillar in a cocoon, I had to change my insides before I could see any real results on the outside. Soon I would shed my cocoon, and I would be free again. That was all I ever wanted anyways, was to be the free and careless girl that I had once been on that beach a few years back. I could do this. With a lot of help from those around me, I got back on my feet. I began to find reasons to fall in love with myself again. Though I had my moments of weakness, in the end I chose to love myself over throwing myself into meaningless relationships like I may have done when I was younger. It took awhile to start enjoying who I was again, and to look forward to each day as it came and went. The struggle was constant but I was persistent. I can't tell you the exact time or place when I realized that I was okay, but when I did realize it, I felt a unique sense of accomplishment that I had looked for and failed to find time and time again.

To this day I still wear the locket that holds the four seashells around my neck. I don't know if it is for comfort or if it's to remember a simpler time in my life. Some days when I'm bored, I take the seashells out and look at them, remembering what happened on those four days during that enchanting summer. I remember the romance, the laughter, and the easiness. I remember the smiles, the joy, and of course the dreams of what was to come. I smile as I remember the Kindred Spirit that brought us all together in the first place. Looking at the seashells I notice that most of them are cracked and some have even broken into a few pieces. It's just like our relationships, they started out perfect to the eye, but eventually the stress wore them down. The important thing to remember though is that there is still something left, something beautiful at that. With certainty I realize that I will always adore those four years that I spent with Victor, and that, that is okay. Our love was timeless, or so it may seem. That's just it though, our love is encapsulated in a time that has past us. This isn't something to mourn over, but rather a memory to celebrate. And finally, I am actually ready to celebrate it.

So I guess our story goes full circle. Morgan and I started off as best friends willing to face the world together. Though we had a dark period where we were apart, Sunset Beach managed to bring us back together somehow. We also met the loves of our lives; and with them fell in and out of love. Those boys are now fortunate enough to be called some of our closest friends. All in all, we broke even, which is all you can really ask for in life to begin with. Although it is over now, I can still look back with a smile on my face and love in my heart, always knowing there will be a special place for him in my heart.

So the question still remains, where do we go from here? I can't say that I know the answer or what the future holds, but still my thoughts stray out to sea.

Via Mary and Morgan
Epilogue
December 1, 2009

Today is a day of celebration because it is the day that we finally finished the book! So where are we now? I, Mary, am a sophomore at Loyola University in MD working on a double degree in Sociology and Theology with a specialization in Special Education. This semester I am out of school due to medical complications but I look forward to going back in the spring. My major is just about the only thing I have decided in my life, as for the rest I'm just taking as it comes, focusing primarily on my health and of course on this book. I spend most of my days finding the little joys and happenstances in life as I finally have time to focus on myself.

I, Morgan, on the other hand am a freshman at University of Maryland, College Park. I am pursuing a degree in Special Education and generally enjoying life. Like Mary, I am just taking life as it comes and enjoying the ride. As for Mary and I together, we are on the road to friendship once more and enjoying ourselves along the way. This book and as we both believe, the Kindred Spirit, brought us back together again and for that we are both so grateful!

And now for the big question, what about the boys? As for Victor, he is in the Air Force on his first real post and is looking forward to a new life in the Military. He is excited for the book to be published and has told Mary time and time again how supportive he is of this whole project. Zack on the other hand is a freshman in college in Pennsylvania and loves it. He has had

183

nothing but positive things to say about the book and is looking forward to reading it when he gets a chance. Both parties are working towards friendship.

Via Mary

I want to thank Victor for the past four years. They were truly amazing. Though I don't know if I could ever have a love like that again, I am grateful that I had what I had, while I had it. Victor, you are truly an amazing man, one of much strength and courage and for that I will forever admire you. It is really important to me that you understand that I am in no way bitter about what happened. I have never learned so much about relationships and about my own capacity to love and be loved until you came into my life.

We gave it our best shot and I firmly believe that we weren't just two naïve teenagers. What we had was rare and was the type of love that people search for their entire lives. Because of you I sincerely understand the meaning and power behind the word "love". Great love awakens the soul to feel every emotion with passion and grace. I truly appreciate all that you have taught me through words and actions. You have helped me grow and become the person I am today. Though it brings me great pain to remember why I am writing this, I understand and in time will come to fully accept why it had to be done. I do believe that we are on the road to friendship and if that's all we'll ever have then so be it. I can't imagine not having you in my life, so thank you again for all four years.

I hope that if we were to see each other in the future that you could look on at me with a smiling face and remember the four years we shared together. I hope when you read this you don't view me as weak but as someone who really cared for you. But most of all, I hope you can walk away from this knowing that when I said I loved you, I meant it with every fiber of my being. You will be in my heart, forever and always.

Via Morgan

Zack. We have been through a lot in the past four years. There is so much that needs to be said. There is nothing that you have done to me that I have not deserved. What I have realized through this whole writing experience is that we both have done things wrong. It was not a one sided affair. I am sorry for the things that I did, and what you did to me I had coming to me. I guess the whole reason for this book was to put the past behind us so that we may be able to be real friends. I don't mean friends that just see each other once a year and talk during football season. I want to have you in my life. I hope that reading this will bring about things about me, and about the situation, that you didn't realize, and I hope that it has helped you to understand me a little bit better. I am not that crazy girl that you think I am, well okay I am but I'm not that crazy.

You will always be something special to me. I hope that you know that. I hope you can see how much of a good thing you were for me, and I want to thank you for that. You may never completely understand but that doesn't matter. I just want you to know that no matter how much this went wrong, I would do it again in a heart beat. I hope that I am not something that you regret and something that you celebrate my memory like I celebrate yours. I just hope that you want to be in my life too. So what do you say, can we be friends? Can we get past this? I am just going to leave this ending up to you. You choose. Do we end like this, or do we continue on as something great, as friends?

Via Victor:

Mary, I'm not exactly sure what you want me to say. I figured talking from the heart would be the best. I still care about you. I hope you are doing well right now. I don't really keep in contact with you too much, but I do still think about you. I'm sorry that things didn't work out, and I don't want you to feel bad but I guess this is all I can do right now. I guess that's about it. I love you guys.

I wish you both the best of luck on this book.

Via Zack

Morgan, the last 4 years have been a great experience. I don't know how different life would be before the summer of 2005, nor do I wish to care. That summer changed my life and I will remember it for the rest of my life. I want to thank you for being a part of that. Life without that summer would feel incomplete. And Mary, you also were a big part in my life. Without you, I feel Morgan and me wouldn't have met and none of this would have happened. Our time at the beach was a great time and I hope to continue to have those great times for years to come. The past four years have been great and I know we can continue to make them better. Without you two, I couldn't imagine what life would be like. Go Steelers.

All in all we are thriving on our own and even when we come together, on that oh so familiar beach each year during the first week in August.

Via Mary
Acknowledgments

First, I want to thank Morgan for collaborating on this project with me. I know she not only put in a lot of hard work. So really I couldn't have asked for a better partner to work with. Hey Morg, we did it!!! Secondly I'd like to thank my grandfather I've probably said it a billion times but without him this story would have never came to be. I'd also like to thank my parents on whom I constantly relied on for love and support while writing. Thank you, Mom and Dad, for putting up with my light on during those late nights of me typing away, I'm sure it wasn't an easy noise to fall asleep to. I want to thank Sara for helping out with the book and helping me with my memories, making sure I had them in order and what not, you are an amazing person and I'm so glad to call you one of my best friends. I'd like to thank all of my other family and friends who were there reading and editing for me as this memoir progressed, I couldn't be more thankful for all of you! I'd like to thank everyone who was involved in creating and publishing this book, your hard work and effort to make everything happen certainly does not go unnoticed, for I am greatly appreciative of all that you have done for me. Lastly, yet certainly not the least, I'd like to thank Victor, without him there would be no story, so thank you for being in my life these past four years, I couldn't ask for anything more!

About the Author

Mary Bosley was born and raised in Reisterstown, MD. She is in her second year and Loyola University in Maryland studying Theology and Sociology with a minor in Special Education. This is Mary's first book, she wrote it because she enjoys writing and storytelling, and hopes that all of you, the readers, had a pleasant time reading it too! When she is not on campus she lives at home with her parents, and older brother, Erik, and their cute black lab, Bailey.

Via Morgan
Acknowledgments

The first and probably most important person I would like to thank would be Mary. Mary, thank you for living this with me. It was a wild ride and I am so glad to have had you by my side through the ups and the lowest of lows. Thank you for being a shoulder to cry on and the support in all of the craziness. Lastly, thank you for pushing me to be the best that I can be, and nudging me to write because it has really helped me in my life to put the past behind me. Next, I would like to thank Zack for the time we spent together. Thank you for being the first positive influence in my life. I still hope that one day we can put the past behind us and actually be friends. I'd like to thank my family and friends for their love and support through all of the hard times. I love you all and you mean the world to me. I would like to thank the readers for listening to my story as well.

About Me

Morgan Przybylski was born and raised in the suburbs of Baltimore, Maryland. She is currently entering into her first year at University of Maryland College Park. Morgan is planning on studying Special Education. She loves to volunteer and likes to be involved in whatever possible. This is Morgan's first book and enjoyed writing it. She enjoys dancing, laughing, and having a good time. When not living in College Park, she lives with her parents, grandparents, older sister, Ashley, younger brother, RJ, and golden retriever, Angeli.